Instant Pot®

FOR BEGINNERS

pil

Publications International, Ltd.

Pictured on the front cover *(clockwise from top left):* Pasta e Ceci *(page 184),* Chocolate Truffle Cake *(page 228),* Sweet Potato and Black Bean Chili *(page 150),* Barbecue Beef Sandwiches *(page 93),* Big Chocolate Chip Cookie *(page 225),* Kale and Roasted Pepper Frittata *(page 14),* Italian Beef Sandwiches *(page 114)* and Tuesday Night Tacos *(page 65).*

Pictured on the back cover *(top to bottom):* Greek Beef Stew *(page 38),* Easy Meatballs *(page 100),* Rich Chocolate Pudding *(page 234),* Beet and Arugula Salad *(page 220)* and Parmesan Potato Wedges *(page 222).*

ISBN: 978-1-64558-730-9

Manufactured in China.

8 7 6 5 4 3 2 1

Microwave Cooking: Microwave ovens vary in wattage. Use the cooking times as guidelines and check for doneness before adding more time.

Instant Pot

TABLE OF CONTENTS

INSTANT POT® 101 _____ 4

BREAKFAST & BRUNCH _____ 10

SOUPS & STEWS _____ 32

POULTRY _____ 64

BEEF _____ 92

PORK _____ 122

BEANS & GRAINS _____ 144

PASTA _____ 174

VEGETABLES _____ 196

DESSERTS _____ 224

PRESSURE COOKING TIMES _____ 248

INDEX _____ 252

Instant Pot

INSTANT POT® 101

WELCOME TO THE WONDERFUL WORLD OF INSTANT POT!

It's not just a myth—the Instant Pot *can* change your life! A kitchen tool that can help you make delicious, homemade, family-friendly meals in a hurry deserves all the fanfare it has received. Discover the great potential of this amazing appliance with this simple beginner's guide and more than 100 mouthwatering recipes.

WHAT EXACTLY IS PRESSURE COOKING?

It's a simple concept: Liquid is heated in a heavy pot with a lid that locks and forms an airtight seal. Since the steam from the hot liquid is trapped inside and can't evaporate, the pressure increases and raises the boiling point of the contents in the pot so these items cook faster at a higher temperature. In general, pressure cooking can reduce cooking time to about one third of the time used in conventional cooking methods—and typically the time spent on pressure cooking is hands off. (There's no peeking or stirring when food is being cooked under pressure.)

WHAT MAKES THE INSTANT POT DIFFERENT?

The Instant Pot is a versatile electric multi-cooker that can be a pressure cooker, rice cooker, slow cooker, steamer and yogurt maker. The cooking programs you'll find on the control panel are convenient shortcuts for some foods you may prepare regularly (rice, beans, etc.) which use preset times and cooking levels. But in these pages we'll explore the basics of pressure cooking with recipes that use the Pressure Cook or Manual button along with customized cooking times and pressure levels. These simple and delicious dishes will inspire you to use your Instant Pot daily and create your own Instant Pot magic!

Tex-Mex Chili (page 112)

One-Pot Pasta with Sausage (page 190)

Fudgy Double Chocolate Brownies (page 244)

INSTANT POT COMPONENTS

The **exterior pot** is where the electrical components are housed. It should never be immersed in water; to clean it, simply unplug the unit, wipe it with a damp cloth and dry it immediately.

The **inner pot** holds the food and fits snugly into the exterior pot. Made of stainless steel, it is removable, and it can be washed by hand or in the dishwasher.

The **LED display** shows a time that indicates where the pressure cooker is in a particular function. The time counts down to zero from the number of minutes that were programmed. (The timing begins once the machine reaches pressure.) For Keep Warm and Yogurt functions, the time counts up.

Instant Pot

The **pressure release valve** is on top of the lid and is used to seal the pot or release steam. To seal the pot, move the valve to the Sealing position; to release pressure, move the valve to the Venting position. This valve can pop off to clean, and to make sure nothing is blocking it.

The **float valve** controls the amount of pressure inside the pressure cooker and indicates when pressure cooking is taking place. The valve rises once the contents of the pot reach working pressure; it drops down when all the pressure has been released after cooking.

The **anti-block shield** is a small stainless steel cage found on the inside of the lid that prevents the pressure cooker from clogging. It can be removed for cleaning.

The **silicone sealing ring** underneath the lid helps create a tight seal to facilitate pressure cooking. The sealing ring has a tendency to absorb strong odors from cooking (particularly from acidic ingredients); washing it regularly with warm soapy water or in the dishwasher will help these odors dissipate, as will storing your Instant Pot with the lid ring side up. If you cook both sweet and savory dishes frequently, you may want to purchase an extra sealing ring (so the scent of curry or pot roast doesn't affect your rice pudding or crème brûlée). Make sure to inspect the ring before cooking—if it has any splits or cracks, it will not work properly and should be replaced.

INSTANT POT COOKING BASICS

Every recipe is slightly different, but most include these basic steps. Read through the entire recipe before beginning to cook so you'll know what ingredients to add and when to add them, which pressure level to use, the cooking time and the release method.

1. Sauté: Many recipes call for sautéing vegetables or browning meat at the beginning of a recipe to add flavor. (Be sure to leave the lid off in this step.)

2. Add the ingredients as the recipe directs and secure the lid, making sure the arrow mark on the lid is aligned with the "close" mark and lock icon on the rim of the outside pot. Turn the pressure release valve to the Sealing position.

3. Select Pressure Cook or Manual, then choose the pressure level. The default setting is high pressure, which is what most recipes in this book use. To change to low pressure, use the Pressure Level or Adjust button. To set the cooking time, use the + and - buttons. The Instant Pot will start automatically.

4. Once the pressure cooking is complete, use the pressure release method directed by the recipe. There are three types of releases:

NATURAL RELEASE:
Let the pressure slowly release on its own, which can take anywhere from 5 to 25 minutes (but is typically in the 10- to 15-minute range). The release time will be shorter for a pot that is less full and longer for one that is more full. When the float valve lowers, the pressure is released and you can open the lid.

QUICK RELEASE:
Use a towel or pot holder to manually turn the pressure valve to the Venting position immediately after the cooking is complete. (Be sure to get out of the way of the steam before turning the valve.) It can take up to 2 minutes to fully release all the pressure; the float valve will drop down when all the pressure is released.

A COMBINATION OF NATURAL AND QUICK RELEASE:
The recipe will instruct you to let the pressure release naturally for a certain amount of time (frequently for 10 minutes), and then do a quick release as directed.

TIPS, TRICKS, DOS AND DON'TS

- Read the manual before beginning. There may be features you won't use, but it will eliminate some beginner's confusion, and it can help you understand how the Instant Pot works—and see all its possibilities. Models also change over time, so the manual can provide the best information about the buttons and functions of your pot. (Note that the terms "Pressure Cook" and "Manual" are interchangeable.)

- Don't overfill the pot—the total amount of food and liquid should not exceed the maximum level marked on the inner pot. Generally it is best not to fill the pot more than two thirds full; when cooking foods that expand during cooking such as beans and grains, do not fill it more than half full.

- Make sure there is always some liquid in the pot before cooking because a minimum amount is required to come up to pressure (the amount differs between models). However, if the recipe contains a large quantity of vegetables or meats, you may be able to use a bit less since these ingredients will create their own liquid.

- Always check that the pressure release valve is in the right position before you start pressure cooking. The food simply won't get cooked if the valve is not in the Sealing position because there will not be enough pressure in the pot.

- Never try to force the lid open after cooking—if the lid won't open, that means the pressure has not fully released. (As a safety feature, the lid remains locked until the float valve drops down.)

- Save the thickeners for after the pressure cooking is done. Pressure cooker recipes often end up with a lot of flavorful liquid left in the pot when cooking is complete; flour or cornstarch mixtures can thicken these liquids into delicious sauces. Use the Sauté function while incorporating the thickeners into the cooking liquid, and then cook and stir until the desired consistency is reached.

- Keep in mind that cooking times in some recipes may vary. We've included pressure cooking time charts as a guide (pages 248–251), but these are approximate times, and numerous variables may cause your results to be different. For example, the freshness of dried beans affects their cooking time (older beans take longer to cook), as does what they are cooked with—hard water (water that is high in mineral content), acidic ingredients, sugar and salt levels can also affect cooking times. So be flexible and experiment with what works best for you—you can always check the doneness of your food and add more time.

- Set reasonable expectations, i.e., don't expect everything you cook in the Instant Pot to be ready in a few minutes. Even though it reduces many conventional cooking times dramatically, nothing is literally "instant"—it will always take time to get up to pressure, and then to release it. (These machines are fast but not magical!)

Instant Pot

BREAKFAST & BRUNCH

PARMESAN GARLIC MONKEY BREAD

makes 6 to 8 servings

2 tablespoons butter, melted

2 tablespoons olive oil

2 cloves garlic, minced

1 teaspoon Italian seasoning

1/4 teaspoon salt

1 cup grated Parmesan cheese (do not use shredded)

1 container (about 16 ounces) refrigerated jumbo biscuits (8 biscuits)

1 cup water

Pizza sauce or marinara sauce (optional)

1. Spray 6-cup bundt pan with nonstick cooking spray. Combine butter, oil, garlic, Italian seasoning and salt in medium bowl; mix well. Place cheese in shallow dish.

2. Separate biscuits; cut each biscuit into quarters. Dip each biscuit piece in butter mixture; roll in cheese to coat. Layer biscuit pieces in prepared pan; cover with foil.

3. Pour water into Instant Pot; place rack in pot. Place pan on rack. Secure lid and move pressure release valve to Sealing position. Press Pressure Cook or Manual; cook at high pressure 25 minutes. Preheat oven to 400°F. Line small baking sheet with foil; spray with cooking spray.

4. When cooking is complete, use natural release for 10 minutes, then release remaining pressure. Remove pan from pot. Uncover; let stand 10 minutes.

5. Invert monkey bread onto prepared baking sheet. Bake about 10 minutes or until top is golden brown. Serve with pizza sauce for dipping, if desired.

11

LEMON BLUEBERRY OATMEAL

makes 4 servings

2 tablespoons butter

1¼ cups steel-cut oats

3¾ cups water

½ teaspoon salt

2 lemons

4 tablespoons honey, divided

¾ cup fresh blueberries

½ cup chopped toasted almonds*

To toast almonds, cook in small skillet over medium heat about 5 minutes or until lightly browned and fragrant, stirring frequently.

1. Press Sauté; melt butter in Instant Pot. Add oats, cook about 6 minutes or until oats are browned and fragrant, stirring frequently. Stir in water and salt; mix well.

2. Secure lid and move pressure release valve to Sealing position. Press Pressure Cook or Manual; cook at high pressure 12 minutes.

3. Grate 4 teaspoons peel from lemons; squeeze 3 tablespoons juice.

4. When cooking is complete, use natural release for 10 minutes, then release remaining pressure. Stir oats until smooth. Add lemon juice, 2 teaspoons grated peel and 2 tablespoons honey; mix well.

5. Top each serving with blueberries, almonds and remaining lemon peel; drizzle with remaining honey.

KALE AND ROASTED PEPPER FRITTATA

makes 6 servings

10 **eggs**

½ **cup whole milk**

1 **teaspoon Greek seasoning**

2 **cups baby kale***

1 **cup (4 ounces) crumbled feta cheese with sun-dried tomatoes and basil**

¾ **cup diced roasted red peppers**

1½ **cups water**

Or substitute 2 cups baby arugula or baby spinach.

1. Spray 1½-quart (6- to 7-inch) soufflé dish with nonstick cooking spray. Beat eggs, milk and Greek seasoning in medium bowl until well blended. Stir in kale, cheese and roasted peppers. Pour into prepared soufflé dish; cover with foil.

2. Pour water into Instant Pot; place rack in pot. Place soufflé dish on rack.

3. Secure lid and move pressure release valve to Sealing position. Press Pressure Cook or Manual; cook at high pressure 30 minutes.

4. When cooking is complete, use natural release for 10 minutes, then release remaining pressure. Remove soufflé dish from pot. Uncover; let stand 5 minutes before serving.

FRENCH TOAST CASSEROLE

makes 6 servings

1 loaf (14 to 16 ounces) day-old cinnamon swirl bread (see Tip)

4 ounces cream cheese, cubed

1½ cups whole milk

4 eggs

¼ cup maple syrup, plus additional for serving

⅛ teaspoon salt

1 cup water

1. Spray 1½-quart (6- to 7-inch) soufflé dish with nonstick cooking spray. Cut bread into 1-inch pieces. (You should have 5 to 6 cups bread cubes.) Place one third of bread in prepared soufflé dish; top with half of cream cheese cubes. Repeat layers; top with remaining bread.

2. Whisk milk, eggs, ¼ cup maple syrup and salt in medium bowl until well blended. Pour over bread and cream cheese; press gently into liquid. Cover with foil; let stand 30 minutes.

3. Pour water into Instant Pot; place rack in pot. Place soufflé dish on rack. Secure lid and move pressure release valve to Sealing position. Press Pressure Cook or Manual; cook at high pressure 35 minutes.

4. When cooking is complete, use natural release for 5 minutes, then release remaining pressure. Remove soufflé dish from pot. Uncover; let stand 5 minutes before serving. Cut into wedges; serve warm with additional maple syrup.

TIP: Day-old bread is drier than fresh bread and better able to absorb the custard mixture in casseroles and bread puddings. If you only have fresh bread, bake the bread cubes on a baking sheet in a 350°F oven about 7 minutes or until lightly toasted.

FRUITY WHOLE GRAIN CEREAL

makes 4 to 6 servings

2¼ cups water

¼ cup steel-cut oats

¼ cup uncooked pearl barley

¼ cup uncooked brown rice

½ teaspoon salt

½ cup milk

⅓ cup golden raisins

¼ cup finely chopped dried dates

¼ cup chopped dried plums

2 tablespoons packed brown sugar

½ teaspoon ground cinnamon

1. Combine water, oats, barley, rice and salt in Instant Pot; mix well.

2. Secure lid and move pressure release valve to Sealing position. Press Pressure Cook or Manual; cook at high pressure 20 minutes.

3. When cooking is complete, use natural release for 10 minutes, then release remaining pressure.

4. Stir in milk, raisins, dates, dried plums, brown sugar and cinnamon; mix well. Serve hot. Refrigerate any leftover cereal in airtight container.

TIP: To reheat cereal, place one serving in microwavable bowl. Microwave on HIGH 30 seconds; stir. Add water or milk to reach desired consistency. Microwave just until hot.

STICKY CINNAMON MONKEY BREAD

makes 6 to 8 servings

⅓ cup sugar

1 tablespoon ground cinnamon

1 container (about 16 ounces) refrigerated jumbo biscuits (8 biscuits)

¼ cup (½ stick) butter, melted

1 cup water

1. Spray 6-cup bundt pan with nonstick cooking spray. Combine sugar and cinnamon in medium bowl; mix well. Sprinkle 1 tablespoon cinnamon-sugar over bottom of prepared pan.

2. Separate biscuits; cut each biscuit into quarters. Dip each biscuit piece in melted butter; roll in remaining cinnamon-sugar to coat. Layer biscuit pieces in prepared pan; cover with foil.

3. Pour water into Instant Pot; place rack in pot. Place pan on rack. Secure lid and move pressure release valve to Sealing position. Press Pressure Cook or Manual; cook at high pressure 25 minutes.

4. When cooking is complete, use natural release for 10 minutes, then release remaining pressure. Remove pan from pot. Uncover; let stand 10 minutes. Invert bread onto plate; serve warm.

APPLE–CINNAMON BREAKFAST RISOTTO

makes 6 servings

- 4 tablespoons (½ stick) butter, divided
- 4 medium Granny Smith apples (about 1½ pounds), peeled and diced
- 1½ teaspoons ground cinnamon, divided
- 1½ cups uncooked arborio rice
- 1 teaspoon salt
- ¼ teaspoon ground allspice
- 4 cups apple juice
- 2 tablespoons packed dark brown sugar, plus additional for serving
- 1 teaspoon vanilla
- Milk, sliced almonds and dried cranberries (optional)

1. Press Sauté; melt 2 tablespoons butter in Instant Pot. Add apples and ½ teaspoon cinnamon; cook and stir about 5 minutes or until apples are softened. Transfer to small bowl; set aside.

2. Melt remaining 2 tablespoons butter in pot. Add rice, remaining 1 teaspoon cinnamon, salt and allspice; cook and stir 1 minute. Stir in apple juice, 2 tablespoons brown sugar and vanilla; mix well.

3. Secure lid and move pressure release valve to Sealing position. Press Pressure Cook or Manual; cook at high pressure 6 minutes.

4. When cooking is complete, use quick release. Press Sauté; add reserved apples to pot. Cook and stir 1 minute or until risotto reaches desired consistency. Serve with milk, almonds, cranberries and additional brown sugar, if desired.

CRUSTLESS SPINACH QUICHE

makes 6 servings

6 **eggs**

¾ **cup half-and-half**

¾ **teaspoon Italian seasoning**

½ **teaspoon salt**

½ **teaspoon black pepper**

1 **package (10 ounces) frozen chopped spinach, thawed and squeezed dry**

1 **cup (4 ounces) shredded Italian cheese blend**

1½ **cups water**

1. Spray 7-inch metal cake pan with nonstick cooking spray. Beat eggs, half-and-half, Italian seasoning, salt and pepper in medium bowl until well blended. Stir in spinach and cheese; mix well. Pour into prepared pan; cover with foil.

2. Pour water into Instant Pot; place rack in pot. Place pan on rack.

3. Secure lid and move pressure release valve to Sealing position. Press Pressure Cook or Manual; cook at high pressure 28 minutes.

4. When cooking is complete, use natural release for 5 minutes, then release remaining pressure. Remove pan from pot. Uncover; let stand 5 minutes before serving.

TIP: To remove the quiche from the pan for serving, run a knife around the edge of the pan to loosen. Invert the quiche onto a plate; invert again onto a second plate. Cut into wedges to serve.

SUPERFOOD BREAKFAST PORRIDGE

makes 4 servings

¾ **cup steel-cut oats**

¼ **cup uncooked quinoa, rinsed and drained**

¼ **cup dried cranberries, plus additional for serving**

¼ **cup raisins**

3 **tablespoons ground flax seeds**

2 **tablespoons chia seeds**

1 **teaspoon olive oil**

¼ **teaspoon salt**

¼ **teaspoon ground cinnamon**

2½ **cups almond milk, plus additional for serving**

1½ **cups water**

Maple syrup (optional)

¼ **cup sliced almonds, toasted* (optional)**

*To toast almonds, cook and stir in small skillet over medium heat 1 to 2 minutes or until lightly browned.

1. Spray heatproof bowl (metal, glass or ceramic) that fits inside of Instant Pot with nonstick cooking spray. Combine oats, quinoa, ¼ cup cranberries, raisins, flax seeds, chia seeds, oil, salt and cinnamon in prepared bowl; mix well. Stir in 2½ cups almond milk until blended.

2. Pour water into pot; place rack in pot. Place bowl on rack. Secure lid and move pressure release valve to Sealing position. Press Pressure Cook or Manual; cook at high pressure 13 minutes.

3. When cooking is complete, use natural release.

4. Stir porridge until smooth. Serve with additional almond milk, cranberries, maple syrup and almonds, if desired.

PANCAKE BREAKFAST CASSEROLE

makes 6 servings

4 eggs

1 cup half-and-half

2 tablespoons sugar

¾ teaspoon ground cinnamon, plus additional for garnish

½ teaspoon vanilla

9 frozen buttermilk pancakes (4-inch diameter), cut in half

1 cup water

Maple syrup

1. Spray 1½-quart (6- to 7-inch) soufflé dish with nonstick cooking spray. Beat eggs, half-and-half, sugar, ¾ teaspoon cinnamon and vanilla in medium bowl until well blended.

2. Arrange 4 or 5 pancake halves standing up around side of prepared soufflé dish. Stack remaining pancake halves in soufflé dish, making layers as even as possible. Pour egg mixture over pancakes; press pancakes gently into liquid. Cover with foil; refrigerate overnight.

3. Remove soufflé dish from refrigerator at least 30 minutes before cooking. Pour water into Instant Pot; place rack in pot. Place soufflé dish on rack. Secure lid and move pressure release valve to Sealing position. Press Pressure Cook or Manual; cook at high pressure 30 minutes.

4. When cooking is complete, use natural release for 5 minutes, then release remaining pressure. Remove soufflé dish from pot. Uncover; sprinkle with additional cinnamon, if desired. Cut into wedges; serve warm with maple syrup.

CLASSIC IRISH OATMEAL

makes 4 servings

2 tablespoons butter

1 cup steel-cut oats

3 cup water

½ teaspoon salt

½ teaspoon ground cinnamon

Berry Compote (optional, recipe follows)

⅓ cup half-and-half

¼ cup packed brown sugar

1. Press Sauté; melt butter in Instant Pot. Add oats; cook about 6 minutes, stirring frequently. Add water, salt and cinnamon; cook and stir 1 minute.

2. Secure lid and move pressure release valve to Sealing position. Press Pressure Cook or Manual; cook at high pressure 13 minutes. Meanwhile, prepare Berry Compote, if desired.

3. When cooking is complete, use natural release for 10 minutes, then release remaining pressure.

4. Stir oats until smooth. Add half-and-half and brown sugar; stir until well blended. If thicker oatmeal is desired, press Sauté and cook 2 to 3 minutes or until desired thickness, stirring constantly. (Oatmeal will also thicken upon standing.) Serve with Berry Compote.

BERRY COMPOTE: Combine 1 cup quartered fresh strawberries, 6 ounces fresh blackberries, 6 ounces fresh blueberries, 3 tablespoons granulated sugar and 1 tablespoon water in medium saucepan; bring to a simmer over medium heat. Cook 8 to 9 minutes or until berries are tender but still hold their shape, stirring occasionally.

Instant Pot

SOUPS & STEWS

CREAMY TOMATO SOUP

makes 6 servings

- 2 tablespoons olive oil
- 2 tablespoons butter
- 1 large onion, finely chopped
- 2 cloves garlic, minced
- 2 teaspoons sugar
- 1½ teaspoons salt
- ½ teaspoon dried oregano
- 2 cans (28 ounces each) peeled Italian plum tomatoes, undrained
  Focaccia Croutons (recipe follows, optional)
- ½ cup whipping cream

1. Press Sauté; heat oil and butter in Instant Pot. Add onion; cook and stir 5 minutes or until softened. Add garlic, sugar, salt and oregano; cook and stir 30 seconds. Stir in tomatoes with juice; mix well.

2. Secure lid and move pressure release valve to Sealing position. Press Pressure Cook or Manual; cook at high pressure 8 minutes. Prepare Focaccia Croutons, if desired.

3. When cooking is complete, use natural release for 10 minutes, then release remaining pressure.

4. Use hand-held immersion blender to blend soup until smooth. Stir in cream until well blended. Serve soup with croutons.

FOCACCIA CROUTONS: Combine 4 cups ½-inch focaccia cubes (half of 9-ounce loaf), 1 tablespoon olive oil and ½ teaspoon black pepper in large bowl; toss to coat. Spread on large baking sheet; bake in preheated 350°F oven about 10 minutes or until golden brown.

SAVORY COD STEW

makes 6 to 8 servings

8 ounces bacon, chopped

1 large onion, diced

1 large carrot, diced

2 stalks celery, diced

2 cloves garlic, minced

1 can (28 ounces) plum tomatoes, undrained, coarsely chopped

2 potatoes, peeled and diced

1 cup clam juice

3 tablespoons tomato paste

3 tablespoons chopped fresh Italian parsley

½ teaspoon salt

¼ teaspoon black pepper

3 saffron threads

2½ pounds fresh cod, skin removed, cut into 1½-inch pieces

1. Press Sauté; cook bacon in Instant Pot until crisp. Drain off all but 2 tablespoons drippings.

2. Add onion, carrot, celery and garlic to pot; cook and stir 5 minutes or until vegetables are softened. Add tomatoes with juice, potatoes, clam juice, tomato paste, parsley, salt, pepper and saffron; cook and stir 2 minutes.

3. Secure lid and move pressure release valve to Sealing position. Press Pressure Cook or Manual; cook at high pressure 2 minutes.

4. When cooking is complete, use quick release. Add cod to pot. Secure lid and move pressure release valve to Sealing position. Press Pressure Cook or Manual; cook at low pressure 1 minute.

5. When cooking is complete, use quick release.

COCONUT CURRY CHICKEN SOUP

makes 4 servings

1 can (about 13 ounces) coconut milk, divided

1½ cups chicken broth

1 cup chopped onion

2 tablespoons curry powder

1 teaspoon salt

½ teaspoon ground ginger

⅛ teaspoon ground red pepper

1½ pounds boneless skinless chicken thighs

¼ cup chopped fresh cilantro or mint

2 cups cooked rice (optional)

Lime wedges (optional)

1. Shake or stir coconut milk until well blended and smooth. Combine half of coconut milk, broth, onion, curry powder, salt, ginger and red pepper in Instant Pot; mix well. Add chicken, pressing into liquid.

2. Secure lid and move pressure release valve to Sealing position. Press Pressure Cook or Manual; cook at high pressure 9 minutes.

3. When cooking is complete, use natural release for 10 minutes, then release remaining pressure. Remove chicken to plate; let stand until cool enough to handle.

4. Shred chicken into bite-size pieces. Press Sauté; add chicken to pot with remaining coconut milk and cilantro. Cook 3 minutes or until heated through, stirring occasionally. Spoon rice over each serving, if desired; serve with lime wedges.

Instant Pot

SOUPS & STEWS

GREEK BEEF STEW

makes 4 to 6 servings

¼ cup all-purpose flour

2 teaspoons Greek seasoning

¼ teaspoon salt

¼ teaspoon black pepper

2 pounds bottom round or boneless beef chuck roast, cut into 1-inch pieces

2 tablespoons olive oil

½ cup beef broth

¼ cup tomato paste

1 pint grape or cherry tomatoes, divided

2 medium onions, each cut into 8 wedges

1 cup pitted kalamata olives

4 sprigs fresh oregano, plus additional for garnish

1 lemon, divided

1. Combine flour, Greek seasoning, salt and pepper in large resealable food storage bag. Add beef; shake to coat.

2. Press Sauté; heat oil in Instant Pot. Cook beef in two batches about 5 minutes or until browned. Remove to plate. Add broth and tomato paste to pot; cook and stir 2 minutes, scraping up browned bits from bottom of pot. Stir in beef, ½ cup grape tomatoes, onions, olives, 4 sprigs oregano and juice of ½ lemon; mix well.

3. Secure lid and move pressure release valve to Sealing position. Press Pressure Cook or Manual; cook at high pressure 20 minutes.

4. When cooking is complete, use natural release for 10 minutes, then release remaining pressure.

5. Press Sauté; add remaining grape tomatoes to pot. Cook about 5 minutes or until tomatoes have softened and stew thickens, stirring frequently. Cut remaining ½ lemon into wedges; serve with stew. Garnish with additional oregano.

CAMPFIRE SAUSAGE AND POTATO SOUP

makes 4 to 6 servings

1 tablespoon olive oil

8 ounces kielbasa sausage, cut in half lengthwise, then cut crosswise into $\frac{1}{2}$-inch slices

1 medium onion, diced

1 teaspoon dried oregano

1 teaspoon ground cumin

1 tablespoon tomato paste

1 large baking potato, peeled and cut into $\frac{1}{2}$-inch cubes

1 can (about 15 ounces) dark red kidney beans, rinsed and drained

1 can (about 14 ounces) diced tomatoes

1 cup beef broth

1 medium green bell pepper, diced

$\frac{1}{4}$ teaspoon salt

1. Press Sauté; heat oil in Instant Pot. Add sausage and onion; cook 5 minutes or until sausage is lightly browned. Add oregano and cumin; cook and stir 30 seconds. Add tomato paste; cook and stir 1 minute. Stir in potato, beans, tomatoes, broth, bell pepper and salt; mix well.

2. Secure lid and move pressure release valve to Sealing position. Press Pressure Cook or Manual; cook at high pressure 3 minutes.

3. When cooking is complete, use natural release for 10 minutes, then release remaining pressure.

SALSA VERDE CHICKEN STEW

makes 4 to 6 servings

2 cans (about 15 ounces each) black beans, rinsed and drained

1½ pounds boneless skinless chicken breasts, cut into 1-inch pieces

1 jar (16 ounces) salsa verde

1½ cups frozen corn

¾ cup chopped fresh cilantro

Diced avocado (optional)

1. Combine beans, chicken and salsa in Instant Pot; mix well.

2. Secure lid and move pressure release valve to Sealing position. Press Pressure Cook or Manual; cook at high pressure 4 minutes.

3. When cooking is complete, use quick release.

4. Press Sauté; add corn to pot. Cook about 3 minutes or until heated through. Stir in cilantro; mix well. Garnish with avocado.

PORK AND CABBAGE SOUP

makes 6 servings

8 ounces pork loin, cut into ½-inch pieces

1 medium onion, chopped

2 slices bacon, finely chopped

1 can (about 28 ounces) whole tomatoes, undrained, coarsely chopped

1 teaspoon salt

1 bay leaf

¾ teaspoon dried marjoram

⅛ teaspoon black pepper

½ medium cabbage, chopped, divided (about 5 cups)

2 medium carrots, cut into ½-inch slices

1 cup chicken broth

2 tablespoons chopped fresh parsley

1. Press Sauté; add pork, onion and bacon to Instant Pot. Cook and stir about 5 minutes or until pork is no longer pink and onion is softened. Add tomatoes with liquid, salt, bay leaf, marjoram and pepper; cook 2 minutes, scraping up browned bits from bottom of pot. Stir in half of cabbage, carrots and broth; mix well.

2. Secure lid and move pressure release valve to Sealing position. Press Pressure Cook or Manual; cook at high pressure 8 minutes.

3. When cooking is complete, use natural release for 10 minutes, then release remaining pressure. Remove and discard bay leaf.

4. Press Sauté; add remaining half of cabbage to pot. Cook about 3 minutes or until cabbage is wilted, stirring frequently. Stir in parsley.

QUICK CHICKEN AND BEAN STEW

makes 4 to 6 servings

1 pound boneless skinless chicken thighs, cut into 1-inch pieces

1 can (about 15 ounces) Great Northern beans, rinsed and drained

1 can (about 15 ounces) black beans, rinsed and drained

1 can (about 14 ounces) crushed tomatoes (preferably fire-roasted)

1 onion, chopped

⅓ cup chicken broth

Juice of 1 large orange (about ⅓ cup)

1 canned chipotle pepper in adobo sauce, minced

1 teaspoon salt

1 teaspoon ground cumin

1 bay leaf

Fresh cilantro sprigs (optional)

1. Combine chicken, beans, tomatoes, onion, broth, orange juice, chipotle pepper, salt, cumin and bay leaf in Instant Pot; mix well.

2. Secure lid and move pressure release valve to Sealing position. Press Pressure Cook or Manual; cook at high pressure 6 minutes.

3. When cooking is complete, use natural release for 5 minutes, then release remaining pressure.

4. Press Sauté; cook 3 to 5 minutes or until stew thickens, stirring frequently. Remove and discard bay leaf. Garnish with cilantro.

MUSHROOM BARLEY SOUP

makes 6 to 8 servings

2 tablespoons olive oil

1 onion, chopped

2 carrots, chopped

2 stalks celery, chopped

3 cloves garlic, minced

1 teaspoon salt

½ teaspoon dried thyme

½ teaspoon black pepper

5 cups vegetable or chicken broth

1 package (16 ounces) sliced mushrooms

½ cup uncooked pearl barley

½ ounce dried porcini or shiitake mushrooms

1. Press Sauté; heat oil in Instant Pot. Add onion, carrots and celery; cook and stir 5 minutes or until vegetables are softened. Add garlic, salt, thyme and pepper; cook and stir 1 minute. Stir in broth, sliced mushrooms, barley and dried mushrooms; mix well.

2. Secure lid and move pressure release valve to Sealing position. Press Pressure Cook or Manual; cook at high pressure 22 minutes.

3. When cooking is complete, use natural release for 10 minutes, then release remaining pressure.

QUICK SHRIMP AND OKRA STEW

makes 4 servings

1 teaspoon vegetable oil

½ cup finely chopped onion

8 ounces okra, ends trimmed, cut into ½-inch slices

1 can (about 14 ounces) whole tomatoes, undrained, chopped

1 teaspoon dried thyme

¾ teaspoon salt

8 ounces medium raw shrimp, peeled and deveined

¾ cup fresh corn or thawed frozen corn

½ teaspoon hot pepper sauce

1. Press Sauté; heat oil in Instant Pot. Add onion; cook and stir 2 minutes or until softened. Add okra; cook and stir 3 minutes. Add tomatoes with juice, thyme and salt; mix well.

2. Secure lid and move pressure release valve to Sealing position. Press Pressure Cook or Manual; cook at high pressure 4 minutes.

3. When cooking is complete, use quick release.

4. Press Sauté; add shrimp, corn and hot pepper sauce to pot. Cook 3 minutes or until shrimp are pink and opaque, stirring frequently.

VEGETABLE BEAN SOUP

makes 6 to 8 servings

1 cup dried Great Northern beans, soaked 8 hours or overnight

1 tablespoon olive oil

1 cup chopped onion

¾ cup chopped carrots

3 cloves garlic, minced

4 cups coarsely chopped green cabbage

4 cups coarsely chopped unpeeled red potatoes (about 4 medium)

1 teaspoon dried rosemary

4 cups vegetable broth

1 can (about 14 ounces) diced tomatoes

1½ teaspoons salt

½ teaspoon black pepper

Grated Parmesan cheese (optional)

1. Rinse and drain beans. Press Sauté; heat oil in Instant Pot. Add onion and carrots; cook and stir 3 minutes or until vegetables are softened. Add garlic; cook and stir 30 seconds. Add cabbage, potatoes and rosemary; cook and stir 1 minute. Stir in beans, broth, tomatoes, salt and pepper; mix well.

2. Secure lid and move pressure release valve to Sealing position. Press Pressure Cook or Manual; cook at high pressure 7 minutes.

3. When cooking is complete, use natural release for 10 minutes, then release remaining pressure. Serve with cheese, if desired.

CURRIED CHICKEN AND WINTER VEGETABLE STEW

makes 4 to 6 servings

1 tablespoon vegetable oil

1 medium onion, chopped

1 tablespoon curry powder

1 clove garlic, minced

1 pound boneless skinless chicken breasts, cut into 1/2-inch pieces

1 can (about 14 ounces) diced tomatoes

1 cup chicken broth

2 medium turnips, cut into 1-inch pieces

2 medium carrots, cut into 1-inch slices

1/2 cup raisins (optional)

1/4 cup tomato paste

1 teaspoon salt

1/8 teaspoon ground red pepper

1. Press Sauté; adjust heat to low. Heat oil in Instant Pot. Add onion; cook and stir 3 minutes or until softened. Add curry powder and garlic; cook and stir 1 minute. Stir in chicken, tomatoes, broth, turnips, carrots, raisins, if desired, tomato paste, salt and red pepper; mix well.

2. Secure lid and move pressure release valve to Sealing position. Press Pressure Cook or Manual; cook at high pressure 5 minutes.

3. When cooking is complete, use natural release for 5 minutes, then release remaining pressure.

SERVING SUGGESTION: Serve with couscous or brown rice.

TURKEY VEGETABLE RICE SOUP

makes 6 to 8 servings

6 cups cold water

2 pounds turkey drumsticks (3 small)

1 large onion, cut into 8 wedges

4 tablespoons soy sauce, divided

1 bay leaf

½ teaspoon salt, divided

½ teaspoon black pepper, divided

2 carrots, sliced

8 ounces mushrooms, sliced

2 cups coarsely chopped bok choy (about 6 ounces)

½ cup uncooked rice

1½ cups fresh snow peas, cut in half crosswise

Sriracha or hot pepper sauce (optional)

1. Combine water, turkey, onion, 2 tablespoons soy sauce, bay leaf, ¼ teaspoon salt and ¼ teaspoon pepper in Instant Pot.

2. Secure lid and move pressure release valve to Sealing position. Press Pressure Cook or Manual; cook at high pressure 25 minutes.

3. When cooking is complete, use natural release for 10 minutes, then release remaining pressure. Remove turkey to plate; let stand until cool enough to handle.

4. Meanwhile, add carrots, mushrooms, bok choy, rice and remaining ¼ teaspoon salt to pot; mix well. Secure lid and move pressure release valve to Sealing position. Press Pressure Cook or Manual; cook at high pressure 4 minutes. When cooking is complete, use natural release for 5 minutes, then release remaining pressure. Remove and discard bay leaf.

5. Remove turkey meat from bones; discard skin and bones. Cut turkey into bite-size pieces. Press Sauté; add turkey, snow peas, remaining 2 tablespoons soy sauce and ¼ teaspoon pepper to pot. Cook 2 to 3 minutes or until snow peas are crisp-tender, stirring occasionally. Serve with sriracha sauce, if desired.

SPLIT PEA SOUP

makes 4 to 6 servings

8 slices bacon, chopped

1 onion, chopped

2 carrots, chopped

1 stalk celery, chopped

1 clove garlic, minced

½ teaspoon dried thyme

1 container (32 ounces) chicken broth

2 cups water

1 package (16 ounces) dried split peas, rinsed and sorted

¾ teaspoon salt

½ teaspoon black pepper

1 bay leaf

1. Press Sauté; cook bacon in Instant Pot until crisp. Remove to paper towel-lined plate. Drain off all but 1 tablespoon drippings.

2. Add onion, carrots and celery to pot; cook and stir 5 minutes or until vegetables are softened. Add garlic and thyme; cook and stir 1 minute. Stir in broth and water, scraping up browned bits from bottom of pot. Add split peas, half of bacon, salt, pepper and bay leaf; mix well.

3. Secure lid and move pressure release valve to Sealing position. Press Pressure Cook or Manual; cook at high pressure 8 minutes.

4. When cooking is complete, use natural release for 10 minutes, then release remaining pressure. Stir soup; remove and discard bay leaf. Garnish with remaining bacon.

NOTE: The soup may seem thin immediately after cooking, but it will thicken upon standing. If prepared in advance and refrigerated, thin the soup with water when reheating until it reaches the desired consistency.

SPICY AFRICAN CHICKPEA AND SWEET POTATO STEW

makes 4 servings

Spice Paste
(recipe follows)

1½ pounds sweet potatoes, peeled and cubed

1 can (about 15 ounces) chickpeas, rinsed and drained

1 can (about 14 ounces) diced tomatoes

1 package (10 ounces) frozen cut okra, thawed (about 2½ cups)

1 cup vegetable broth or water

Hot cooked couscous or rice (optional)

Hot pepper sauce (optional)

Fresh cilantro sprigs (optional)

1. Prepare Spice Paste.

2. Combine sweet potatoes, chickpeas, tomatoes, okra, broth and Spice Paste in Instant Pot; mix well.

3. Secure lid and move pressure release valve to Sealing position. Press Pressure Cook or Manual; cook at high pressure 3 minutes.

4. When cooking is complete, use quick release. Serve stew with couscous and hot pepper sauce, if desired. Garnish with cilantro.

SPICE PASTE: Combine 6 cloves peeled garlic and 1 teaspoon salt in blender or small food processor; blend until garlic is finely chopped. Add 2 teaspoons paprika, 1½ teaspoons cumin seeds, 1 teaspoon black pepper, ½ teaspoon ground ginger and ½ teaspoon ground allspice; process 15 seconds. With blender running, pour 1 tablespoon olive oil through opening in cover; blend until mixture forms paste.

ONE–POT CHINESE CHICKEN SOUP

makes 4 servings

1 container (32 ounces) chicken broth

⅓ cup reduced-sodium soy sauce

1 pound boneless skinless chicken thighs

1 package (16 ounces) frozen stir-fry vegetables (do not thaw)

6 ounces uncooked thin Chinese egg noodles

1 to 3 tablespoons sriracha sauce

1. Combine broth and soy sauce in Instant Pot; mix well. Add chicken. Secure lid and move pressure release valve to Sealing position. Press Pressure Cook or Manual; cook at high pressure 8 minutes.

2. When cooking is complete, use quick release. Remove chicken to bowl; set aside 5 minutes or until cool enough to handle. Shred chicken into bite-size pieces.

3. Press Sauté; add vegetables and noodles to broth mixture in pot. Cook about 3 minutes or until noodles are tender. Stir in chicken and 1 tablespoon sriracha sauce; taste and add additional sauce for a spicier flavor.

Instant Pot

POULTRY

TUESDAY NIGHT TACOS

1 tablespoon vegetable oil

1½ pounds boneless skinless chicken thighs

1 cup chunky salsa

Corn tortillas, warmed

½ cup shredded lettuce

1 cup pico de gallo

1 cup (4 ounces) shredded taco blend or Cheddar cheese

Lime wedges (optional)

Optional toppings: sour cream, sliced jalapeño peppers, pickled onions and/or diced avocado

1. Press Sauté; heat oil in Instant Pot. Add chicken; cook 5 minutes or until browned on both sides. Add salsa; cook 1 minute, scraping up browned bits from bottom of pot. Turn chicken to coat with salsa.

2. Secure lid and move pressure release valve to Sealing position. Press Pressure Cook or Manual; cook at high pressure 11 minutes.

3. When cooking is complete, use quick release. Use two forks or tongs to shred chicken into bite-size pieces in pot.

4. Serve chicken mixture in tortillas with lettuce, pico de gallo, cheese and lime wedges, if desired. Top as desired.

ROTISSERIE–STYLE CHICKEN

makes 4 servings

1 whole chicken
   (about
   4 pounds)
2 tablespoons rotisserie
   chicken seasoning
   (see Tip)
1 tablespoon butter
1 tablespoon olive oil
1 cup chicken broth
   Fresh parsley sprigs
   and lemon wedges
   (optional)

1. Pat chicken dry. Tie drumsticks together with kitchen string and tuck wing tips under. Sprinkle seasoning inside cavity and over all sides of chicken, pressing to adhere.

2. Press Sauté; heat butter and oil in Instant Pot. Add chicken, breast side up; cook about 5 minutes or until browned. Turn chicken over using tongs and spatula; cook about 5 minutes or until browned. Remove chicken to plate.

3. Add broth to pot; cook 1 minute, scraping up browned bits from bottom of pot. Place rack in pot; place chicken on rack, breast side up.

4. Secure lid and move pressure release valve to Sealing position. Press Pressure Cook or Manual; cook at high pressure 21 minutes.

5. When cooking is complete, use natural release for 15 minutes, then release remaining pressure. Remove chicken to cutting board; tent with foil and let stand 10 minutes before carving. If desired, strain cooking liquid and serve with chicken. Garnish with parsley and lemon wedges.

TIP: Rotisserie chicken seasoning is available in the spice section of many supermarkets. If unavailable, use a basic poultry seasoning or Italian seasoning combined with 1 teaspoon salt and 1 teaspoon paprika. Or use your favorite seasoning blend.

NOTE: When fully cooked, the temperature of the chicken (tested in the thigh) should be 165°F. A chicken larger than 4 pounds may take an additional 3 minutes to cook, while a smaller chicken will take a few minutes less.

PESTO TURKEY MEATBALLS

makes 4 servings

- 1 pound ground turkey
- $1/3$ cup pesto sauce
- $1/3$ cup grated Parmesan cheese, plus additional for garnish
- $1/4$ cup panko bread crumbs
- 1 egg
- 2 green onions, finely chopped
- $1/2$ teaspoon salt, divided
- 2 tablespoons olive oil
- 2 cloves garlic, minced
- $1/8$ teaspoon red pepper flakes
- 1 can (28 ounces) whole tomatoes, undrained, crushed with hands or coarsely chopped
- 1 tablespoon tomato paste
- Hot cooked pasta (optional)
- Chopped fresh basil (optional)

1. Combine turkey, pesto, $1/3$ cup cheese, panko, egg, green onions and $1/4$ teaspoon salt in medium bowl; mix well. Shape mixture into 24 ($1\frac{1}{4}$-inch) meatballs. Refrigerate meatballs while preparing sauce.

2. Press Sauté; heat oil in Instant Pot. Add garlic and red pepper flakes; cook and stir 1 minute. Add tomatoes with liquid, tomato paste and remaining $1/4$ teaspoon salt; cook 3 minutes or until sauce begins to simmer, stirring occasionally.

3. Remove about 1 cup sauce from pot. Arrange meatballs in single layer in pot; pour reserved sauce over meatballs.

4. Secure lid and move pressure release valve to Sealing position. Press Pressure Cook or Manual; cook at high pressure 10 minutes.

5. When cooking is complete, use natural release for 10 minutes, then release remaining pressure. If sauce is too thin, press Sauté and cook 5 minutes or until sauce thickens, stirring frequently. Serve meatballs over pasta, if desired. Garnish with additional cheese and basil.

BUTTER CHICKEN

2 tablespoons butter

1 onion, chopped

4 cloves garlic, minced

1 teaspoon minced
   fresh ginger

1 teaspoon ground
   turmeric

1 teaspoon ground
   coriander

1 teaspoon garam masala

1 teaspoon ground cumin

½ teaspoon ground
   red pepper

½ teaspoon paprika

1 can (about 14 ounces)
   diced tomatoes

¾ teaspoon salt

2 pounds boneless
   skinless chicken
   breasts, cut into
   2-inch pieces

½ cup whipping cream

   Chopped fresh cilantro

   Hot cooked rice (optional)

1. Press Sauté; melt butter in Instant Pot. Add onion; cook and stir about 4 minutes or until onion begins to turn golden. Add garlic and ginger; cook and stir 1 minute. Add turmeric, coriander, garam masala, cumin, red pepper and paprika; cook and stir 30 seconds. Add tomatoes and salt; cook and stir 2 minutes. Stir in chicken; mix well.

2. Secure lid and move pressure release valve to Sealing position. Press Pressure Cook or Manual; cook at high pressure 8 minutes.

3. When cooking is complete, use natural release for 10 minutes, then release remaining pressure.

4. Press Sauté; adjust heat to low. Stir in cream; cook 5 minutes or until heated through. Sprinkle with cilantro; serve with rice, if desired.

HEARTY CHICKEN CHILI

makes 4 servings

1 tablespoon vegetable oil

1 onion, finely chopped

1 jalapeño pepper,* minced

1 clove garlic, minced

1½ teaspoons chili powder

¾ teaspoon salt

½ teaspoon ground cumin

½ teaspoon dried oregano

½ teaspoon black pepper

¼ teaspoon red pepper flakes (optional)

1 cup chicken broth

1½ pounds boneless skinless chicken thighs, cut into 1-inch pieces

2 cans (about 15 ounces each) hominy, rinsed and drained

1 can (about 15 ounces) pinto beans, rinsed and drained

1 tablespoon all-purpose flour (optional)

Chopped fresh cilantro (optional)

Jalapeño peppers can sting and irritate the skin, so wear rubber gloves when handling peppers and do not touch your eyes.

1. Press Sauté; heat oil in Instant Pot. Add onion; cook and stir 3 minutes or until softened. Add jalapeño, garlic, chili powder, salt, cumin, oregano, black pepper and red pepper flakes, if desired; cook and stir 30 seconds. Stir in broth; cook 1 minute. Add chicken, hominy and beans; mix well.

2. Secure lid and move pressure release valve to Sealing position. Press Pressure Cook or Manual; cook at high pressure 6 minutes.

3. When cooking is complete, use natural release for 10 minutes, then release remaining pressure.

4. For thicker chili, stir 1 tablespoon flour into 3 tablespoons cooking liquid in small bowl until smooth. Press Sauté; add flour mixture to chili. Cook about 5 minutes or until chili thickens, stirring occasionally. Garnish with cilantro.

CHICKEN ADOBO

makes 4 servings

⅓ cup cider vinegar

⅓ cup reduced-sodium
 soy sauce

5 cloves garlic, minced

3 bay leaves

1 teaspoon black pepper

2½ pounds bone-in skin-on
 chicken thighs
 (about 6)

 Hot cooked rice (optional)

 Sliced green onion
 (optional)

1. Combine vinegar, soy sauce, garlic, bay leaves and pepper in Instant Pot; mix well. Add chicken; turn to coat. Arrange chicken skin side down in liquid.

2. Secure lid and move pressure release valve to Sealing position. Press Pressure Cook or Manual; cook at high pressure 13 minutes. Preheat broiler. Line baking sheet with foil.

3. When cooking is complete, use natural release for 10 minutes, then release remaining pressure. Remove chicken to prepared baking sheet, skin side up.

4. Broil about 4 minutes or until skin is browned and crisp. Meanwhile, press Sauté; cook liquid in pot about 5 minutes or until slightly reduced. Serve sauce over chicken and rice, if desired. Garnish with green onion.

HOISIN BARBECUE CHICKEN SLIDERS

makes 16 sliders

⅔ **cup hoisin sauce**

⅓ **cup barbecue sauce**

1 **tablespoon soy sauce**

¼ **teaspoon red pepper flakes**

3 to 3½ **pounds boneless skinless chicken thighs**

2 **tablespoons water**

1 **tablespoon cornstarch**

16 **dinner rolls or Hawaiian sweet rolls, split**

½ **medium red onion, finely chopped**

Sliced pickles (optional)

1. Combine hoisin sauce, barbecue sauce, soy sauce and red pepper flakes in Instant Pot; mix well. Add chicken; stir to coat.

2. Secure lid and move pressure release valve to Sealing position. Press Pressure Cook or Manual; cook at high pressure 8 minutes.

3. When cooking is complete, use natural release for 5 minutes, then release remaining pressure. Remove chicken to large plate; let stand until cool enough to handle. Shred chicken into bite-size pieces.

4. Stir water into cornstarch in small bowl until smooth. Press Sauté; add cornstarch mixture to pot. Cook and stir about 2 minutes or until sauce thickens. Return chicken to pot; mix well. Spoon about ¼ cup chicken onto each roll; serve with onion and pickles, if desired.

SPANISH CHICKEN AND RICE

makes 6 servings

- 2 tablespoons olive oil
- 1 package (about 12 ounces) kielbasa sausage, cut into ½-inch slices
- 2 pounds boneless skinless chicken thighs (about 6)
- 1 onion, chopped
- 4 cloves garlic, minced
- 2 cups uncooked converted long grain rice
- 1 red bell pepper, diced
- ½ cup diced carrots
- ¾ teaspoon salt
- ¼ teaspoon black pepper
- ¼ teaspoon saffron threads (optional)
- 3 cups chicken broth
- ½ cup thawed frozen peas

1. Press Sauté; heat oil in Instant Pot. Add sausage; cook about 6 minutes or until browned. Remove to plate. Add chicken to pot in batches; cook about 8 minutes or until browned on both sides. Remove to plate.

2. Add onion to pot; cook and stir 3 minutes or until softened. Add garlic; cook and stir 30 seconds. Add rice, bell pepper, carrots, salt, black pepper and saffron, if desired; cook and stir 3 minutes. Stir in broth, scraping up browned bits from bottom of pot. Return chicken and sausage to pot, pressing chicken into liquid.

3. Secure lid and move pressure release valve to Sealing position. Press Pressure Cook or Manual; cook at high pressure 7 minutes.

4. When cooking is complete, use quick release. Remove chicken to clean plate; tent with foil.

5. Stir peas into rice mixture; cover and let stand 2 minutes or until peas are heated through. Serve chicken over rice mixture.

INDIAN–STYLE APRICOT CHICKEN

makes 4 to 6 servings

2½ **pounds bone-in chicken thighs, skin removed**

½ **teaspoon salt**

¼ **teaspoon black pepper**

1 **tablespoon vegetable oil**

1 **large onion, chopped**

½ **cup chicken broth, divided**

1 **tablespoon grated fresh ginger**

2 **cloves garlic, minced**

½ **teaspoon ground cinnamon**

⅛ **teaspoon ground allspice**

1 **can (about 14 ounces) diced tomatoes**

1 **package (8 ounces) dried apricots**

Pinch saffron threads (optional)

Hot cooked basmati rice (optional)

Chopped fresh Italian parsley (optional)

1. Season both sides of chicken with ½ teaspoon salt and ¼ teaspoon pepper. Press Sauté; heat oil in Instant Pot. Add chicken in batches; cook about 8 minutes or until browned on both sides. Remove to plate.

2. Add onion and 2 tablespoons broth to pot; cook and stir 5 minutes or until onion is translucent, scraping up browned bits from bottom of pot. Add ginger, garlic, cinnamon and allspice; cook and stir 30 seconds or until fragrant. Stir in tomatoes, apricots, remaining broth and saffron, if desired; mix well. Return chicken to pot, pressing into liquid.

3. Secure lid and move pressure release valve to Sealing position. Press Pressure Cook or Manual; cook at high pressure 11 minutes.

4. When cooking is complete, use quick release. Season with additional salt and pepper. Serve with rice, if desired. Garnish with parsley.

HERB LEMON TURKEY BREAST

makes 4 servings

½ cup lemon juice

½ cup dry white wine

4 cloves garlic, minced

1 teaspoon salt

½ teaspoon dried parsley
  flakes

½ teaspoon dried tarragon

½ teaspoon dried rosemary

¼ teaspoon ground sage

¼ teaspoon black pepper

1 boneless turkey breast
  (about 3 pounds)

  Fresh rosemary sprigs
  and lemon slices
  (optional)

1. Combine lemon juice, wine, garlic, salt, parsley flakes, tarragon, dried rosemary, sage and pepper in measuring cup or small bowl; mix well.

2. Place turkey breast in Instant Pot; pour juice mixture over turkey, turning to coat. (Turkey should be skin side up for cooking.)

3. Secure lid and move pressure release valve to Sealing position. Press Pressure Cook or Manual; cook at high pressure 30 minutes.

4. When cooking is complete, use natural release for 10 minutes, then release remaining pressure. Remove turkey to cutting board; tent with foil. Let stand 10 minutes before slicing.

5. Use cooking liquid as sauce, if desired, or thicken liquid with flour (see Tip). Garnish as desired.

TIP: If desired, prepare gravy with cooking liquid after removing turkey from pot. Place ¼ cup all-purpose flour in small bowl; stir in ½ cup cooking liquid from pot until smooth. Press Sauté; add flour mixture to pot. Cook 5 minutes or until gravy thickens, stirring frequently.

ARTICHOKE DIJON CHICKEN THIGHS

makes 4 to 6 servings

1 jar (12 ounces) quartered marinated artichoke hearts, undrained

⅓ cup Dijon mustard

2 tablespoons minced garlic

½ teaspoon dried tarragon

¼ teaspoon salt

2½ pounds bone-in chicken thighs, skin removed

1½ cups thickly sliced mushrooms

1 cup chopped onion

2 tablespoons water

1 tablespoon all-purpose flour

¼ cup chopped fresh parsley

Hot cooked pasta (optional)

1. Drain artichokes, reserving ½ cup marinade. Discard remaining marinade. Combine reserved marinade, mustard, garlic, tarragon and salt in Instant Pot; mix well. Add chicken, mushrooms and onion; stir to coat.

2. Secure lid and move pressure release valve to Sealing position. Press Pressure Cook or Manual; cook at high pressure 11 minutes. When cooking is complete, use natural release for 10 minutes, then release remaining pressure.

3. Remove chicken to plate; tent with foil. Press Sauté; add artichokes to pot. Cook about 5 minutes or until sauce is reduced by half and artichokes are heated through, stirring occasionally.

4. Stir water into flour in small bowl until smooth. Add to sauce; cook and stir 1 minute or until sauce thickens. Stir in parsley. Serve chicken and sauce over pasta, if desired.

CHIPOTLE BBQ
TURKEY SANDWICHES

makes 4 servings

1 tablespoon vegetable oil

1 small red onion, chopped

½ teaspoon chipotle
chili powder

¾ cup plus 2 tablespoons
barbecue sauce,
divided

1 package (24 ounces)
turkey tenderloins
(2 tenderloins), each
cut in half

4 sandwich buns

1. Press Sauté; heat oil in Instant Pot. Add onion; cook and stir 3 minutes or until softened. Add chili powder; cook and stir 30 seconds. Stir in ¾ cup barbecue sauce; mix well. Add turkey; turn to coat.

2. Secure lid and move pressure release valve to Sealing position. Press Pressure Cook or Manual; cook at high pressure 20 minutes.

3. When cooking is complete, use natural release for 10 minutes, then release remaining pressure. Remove turkey to large bowl; let stand 5 minutes. Shred turkey into bite-size pieces.

4. Meanwhile, press Sauté; adjust heat to low. Cook sauce 5 minutes or until slightly reduced. Add shredded turkey and remaining 2 tablespoons barbecue sauce to pot; cook 2 minutes, stirring frequently. Serve on buns.

Instant Pot
POULTRY

PROVENÇAL LEMON AND OLIVE CHICKEN

makes 4 servings

2 cups chopped onions

2½ pounds bone-in chicken thighs, skin removed

1 lemon, thinly sliced and seeded

1 cup pitted green olives

1 tablespoon olive brine or white vinegar

2 teaspoons herbes de Provence*

1 bay leaf

1 teaspoon salt

¼ teaspoon black pepper

⅓ cup chicken broth

½ cup minced fresh Italian parsley

Hot cooked rice (optional)

Or substitute ½ teaspoon each dried rosemary, thyme, sage and savory.

1. Place onions in Instant Pot. Arrange chicken over onions; top with lemon slices. Add olives, brine, herbes de Provence, bay leaf, salt and pepper. Pour in broth.

2. Secure lid and move pressure release valve to Sealing position. Press Pressure Cook or Manual; cook at high pressure 10 minutes.

3. When cooking is complete, use quick release. Remove chicken to plate; tent with foil.

4. Press Sauté; cook about 5 minutes or until sauce is reduced by one third. Remove and discard bay leaf; stir in parsley. Serve sauce with chicken and rice, if desired.

CHICKEN ENCHILADA CHILI

makes 4 servings

1 can (about 14 ounces) diced tomatoes with green chiles

1 can (10 ounces) red enchilada sauce

½ teaspoon salt

¼ teaspoon ground cumin

⅛ teaspoon black pepper

1½ pounds boneless skinless chicken thighs, cut into 1-inch pieces

1 cup frozen or canned corn

1½ tablespoons cornmeal

2 tablespoons finely chopped fresh cilantro

½ cup (2 ounces) shredded pepper jack cheese

Sliced green onions (optional)

1. Combine tomatoes, enchilada sauce, salt, cumin and pepper in Instant Pot; mix well. Add chicken; stir to coat.

2. Secure lid and move pressure release valve to Sealing position. Press Pressure Cook or Manual; cook at high pressure 5 minutes.

3. When cooking is complete, use natural release for 10 minutes, then release remaining pressure.

4. Press Sauté; add corn and cornmeal to pot. Cook about 6 minutes or until chili thickens, stirring frequently. Stir in cilantro. Sprinkle with cheese; garnish with green onions.

Instant Pot

BEEF

BARBECUE BEEF SANDWICHES

2½ pounds boneless beef chuck roast, cut in half

2 tablespoons Southwest seasoning

1 tablespoon vegetable oil

½ cup beef broth

1½ cups barbecue sauce, divided

4 sandwich or pretzel buns, split

1⅓ cups prepared coleslaw* (preferably vinegar based)

Vinegar-based coleslaws provide a perfect complement to the rich beef; they can often be found at the salad bar, deli counter or prepared foods section of large supermarkets.

1. Sprinkle both sides of beef with Southwest seasoning. Press Sauté; heat oil in Instant Pot. Add beef; cook about 6 minutes per side or until browned. Remove to plate.

2. Add broth to pot; cook 2 minutes, scraping up browned bits from bottom of pot. Stir in ½ cup barbecue sauce. Return beef to pot; turn to coat.

3. Secure lid and move pressure release valve to Sealing position. Press Pressure Cook or Manual; cook at high pressure 60 minutes.

4. When cooking is complete, use natural release for 15 minutes, then release remaining pressure. Remove beef to large bowl; let stand until cool enough to handle. Shred beef into bite-size pieces. Stir in remaining 1 cup barbecue sauce.

5. Fill buns with beef mixture; top with coleslaw.

TACO SALAD

makes 4 servings

CHILI

- 1 pound ground beef
- 1 medium onion, chopped
- 1 stalk celery, chopped
- 2 medium tomatoes, chopped
- 1 jalapeño pepper,*
  finely chopped
- 1½ teaspoons chili powder
- 1 teaspoon salt
- 1 teaspoon ground cumin
- ½ teaspoon black pepper
- 1 can (15 ounces) tomato
  sauce
- 1 can (about 15 ounces) kidney
  beans, rinsed and drained
- 1 can (about 15 ounces) pinto
  beans, rinsed and drained
- ½ cup water

SALAD

- 8 cups chopped romaine
  lettuce (large pieces)
- 2 cups diced fresh tomatoes
- 2 cups small tortilla chips
  Optional toppings: salsa,
  sour cream, shredded
  Cheddar cheese

*Jalapeño peppers can sting and
irritate the skin, so wear rubber
gloves when handling peppers
and do not touch your eyes.*

1. Press Sauté; add beef to Instant Pot. Cook about 8 minutes or until browned, stirring frequently. Drain off fat and excess liquid. Add onion and celery to pot; cook and stir 3 minutes.

2. Add chopped tomatoes, jalapeño, chili powder, salt, cumin and black pepper; cook and stir 1 minute. Stir in tomato sauce, beans and water; mix well.

3. Secure lid and move pressure release valve to Sealing position. Press Pressure Cook or Manual; cook at high pressure 20 minutes.

4. When cooking is complete, use natural release for 10 minutes, then release remaining pressure.

5. For each salad, combine 2 cups lettuce and ½ cup diced tomatoes in individual bowl. Top with tortilla chips, chili, salsa, sour cream and cheese, if desired. (Recipe makes more chili than needed for salads; reserve remaining chili for another use.)

ITALIAN BEEF RAGU

makes 6 servings

2 pounds boneless beef chuck roast, cut into 2-inch pieces

½ teaspoon salt

½ teaspoon black pepper

1 tablespoon olive oil

1 onion, chopped

½ cup plus 2 tablespoons beef broth, divided

1 jar (24 ounces) garlic and herb pasta sauce

¼ cup plus 1 tablespoon red wine vinegar, divided

Hot cooked pappardelle pasta

Slivered fresh basil (optional)

Grated Parmesan cheese (optional)

1. Season beef with ½ teaspoon salt and ½ teaspoon pepper. Press Sauté; heat oil in Instant Pot. Add beef in two batches; cook about 5 minutes or until browned. Remove to plate. Add onion and 2 tablespoons broth to pot; cook 3 minutes or until softened, scraping up browned bits from bottom of pot. Reserve ¾ cup pasta sauce; set aside. Add remaining pasta sauce, ½ cup broth and ¼ cup vinegar to pot; mix well. Return beef and accumulated juices to pot; stir to coat.

2. Secure lid and move pressure release valve to Sealing position. Press Pressure Cook or Manual; cook at high pressure 45 minutes.

3. When cooking is complete, use natural release 15 minutes, then release remaining pressure. Remove beef to large bowl; let stand 5 minutes or until cool enough to handle.

4. Meanwhile, press Sauté; adjust heat to low. Add reserved ¾ cup pasta sauce and remaining 1 tablespoon vinegar to pot; cook 5 minutes, stirring occasionally.

5. Shred beef into bite-size pieces; stir into sauce. Taste and season with additional salt and pepper. Serve over pasta; garnish with basil and cheese.

CREOLE–SPICED POT ROAST

2 tablespoons Creole or Cajun seasoning

1 boneless beef chuck roast (3 pounds), cut in half

1 tablespoon vegetable oil

1 medium onion, chopped

1 can (about 14 ounces) diced tomatoes, drained

1 can (about 14 ounces) diced tomatoes with mild green chiles, drained

2 tablespoons hot pepper sauce

1 teaspoon sugar

½ teaspoon black pepper

1 cup chopped rutabaga

1 cup chopped mushrooms

1 cup chopped turnip

1 cup chopped parsnip

1 cup chopped green bell pepper

1 cup green beans (2-inch pieces)

1 cup sliced carrots

1 cup corn

1. Rub Creole seasoning into all sides of beef. Press Sauté; heat oil in Instant Pot. Add beef; cook about 10 minutes or until browned on all sides. Add onion to pot during last few minutes of cooking, stirring until softened. Add tomatoes, hot pepper sauce, sugar and black pepper; mix well.

2. Secure lid and move pressure release valve to Sealing position. Press Pressure Cook or Manual; cook at high pressure 65 minutes.

3. When cooking is complete, use quick release. Add rutabaga, mushrooms, turnip, parsnip, bell pepper, beans, carrots and corn to pot, pressing vegetables down into liquid.

4. Secure lid and move pressure release valve to Sealing position. Press Pressure Cook or Manual; cook at high pressure 10 minutes.

5. When cooking is complete, use quick release.

EASY MEATBALLS

makes 4 servings

1 pound ground beef

1 egg, beaten

3 tablespoons Italian-seasoned dry bread crumbs

1 clove garlic, minced

1 teaspoon dried oregano

¾ teaspoon salt

¼ teaspoon black pepper

⅛ teaspoon ground red pepper

3 cups marinara or tomato-basil pasta sauce

Hot cooked spaghetti

Slivered fresh basil (optional)

Grated Parmesan cheese (optional)

1. Combine beef, egg, bread crumbs, garlic, oregano, salt, black pepper and red pepper in medium bowl; mix gently. Shape into 16 (1½-inch) meatballs.

2. Pour marinara sauce into Instant Pot. Add meatballs to sauce; turn to coat and submerge meatballs in sauce.

3. Secure lid and move pressure release valve to Sealing position. Press Pressure Cook or Manual; cook at high pressure 8 minutes.

4. When cooking is complete, use quick release. Serve meatballs and sauce over spaghetti; top with basil and cheese, if desired.

BACON AND STOUT SHORT RIBS

makes 4 to 6 servings

6 slices thick-cut bacon, chopped

4 pounds bone-in beef short ribs, trimmed and cut into 3-inch pieces

1 teaspoon salt, divided

½ teaspoon black pepper

1 large onion, cut in half and thinly sliced

1 tablespoon tomato paste

1 bottle or can (12 ounces) stout, dark beer or ale

2 tablespoons spicy brown mustard

1 bay leaf

3 tablespoons water

2 tablespoons all-purpose flour

2 tablespoons finely chopped fresh parsley

Hot mashed potatoes or cooked egg noodles (optional)

1. Press Sauté; cook bacon in Instant Pot until crisp. Remove to paper towel-lined plate. Drain off all but 1 tablespoon drippings.

2. Season short ribs with ½ teaspoon salt and pepper. Add short ribs to pot in batches; cook about 8 minutes or until browned on all sides. Remove to plate. Drain off all but 1 tablespoon fat.

3. Add onion to pot; cook and stir 5 minutes or until golden brown. Add tomato paste; cook and stir 1 minute. Add stout, mustard, bay leaf and remaining ½ teaspoon salt; cook and stir 1 minute, scraping up browned bits from bottom of pot. Return bacon and short ribs to pot.

4. Secure lid and move pressure release valve to Sealing position. Press Pressure Cook or Manual; cook at high pressure 45 minutes.

5. When cooking is complete, use natural release for 10 minutes, then release remaining pressure. Remove short ribs to clean plate; tent with foil. Remove and discard bay leaf.

6. Skim excess fat from surface of sauce. Stir water into flour in small bowl until smooth. Press Sauté; add flour mixture to cooking liquid in pot, stirring constantly. Cook and stir about 5 minutes or until sauce thickens. Stir in parsley. Serve sauce with short ribs and mashed potatoes, if desired.

BEEF

BEEF STEW WITH A COFFE

⅓ cup all-purpose flour

1 teaspoon salt

1 teaspoon dried marjoram

½ teaspoon garlic powder

½ teaspoon black pepper

2 pounds beef stew meat, cut into 1-inch pieces

2 tablespoons vegetable oil

3 small onions, cut into wedges

¾ cup strong brewed coffee, at room temperature

1 can (about 14 ounces) diced tomatoes

1 bay leaf

2 cups diced peeled potatoes (½-inch pieces)

4 stalks celery, cut into ½-inch slices

4 medium carrots, cut into ½-inch slices

1. Combine flour, salt, marjoram, garlic powder and pepper in large resealable food storage bag. Add beef; toss to coat.

2. Press Sauté; heat oil in Instant Pot. Add beef in two batches; cook about 5 minutes or until browned. Remove to plate.

3. Add onions to pot; cook and stir 3 minutes or until softened. Add coffee; cook and stir 1 minute, scraping up browned bits from bottom of pot. Return beef to pot with tomatoes and bay leaf; mix well.

4. Secure lid and move pressure release valve to Sealing position. Press Pressure Cook or Manual; cook at high pressure 25 minutes.

5. When cooking is complete, use natural release for 5 minutes, then release remaining pressure. Add potatoes, celery and carrots to pot. Secure lid and move pressure release valve to Sealing position. Press Pressure Cook or Manual; cook at high pressure 12 minutes.

6. When cooking is complete, use quick release. Remove and discard bay leaf. Let stew cool in pot 5 minutes, stirring occasionally. (Stew will thicken as it cools.)

SIMPLE SLOPPY JOES

makes 6 servings

1½ pounds ground beef

1 red bell pepper, chopped

½ cup chopped onion

1 clove garlic, minced

¼ cup ketchup

¼ cup barbecue sauce

2 tablespoons cider vinegar

1 tablespoon Worcestershire sauce

1 tablespoon packed brown sugar

1 teaspoon chili powder

1 can (about 8 ounces) baked beans

6 sandwich rolls, split

¾ cup (3 ounces) shredded Cheddar cheese (optional)

1. Press Sauté; add beef to Instant Pot. Cook about 8 minutes or until browned, stirring frequently. Drain off fat and excess liquid. Add bell pepper, onion and garlic to pot; cook and stir 3 minutes. Add ketchup, barbecue sauce, vinegar, Worcestershire sauce, brown sugar and chili powder; mix well.

2. Secure lid and move pressure release valve to Sealing position. Press Pressure Cook or Manual; cook at high pressure 10 minutes.

3. When cooking is complete, use quick release. Press Sauté; add beans to pot. Cook 5 minutes or until beef mixture thickens, stirring frequently.

4. Serve beef mixture on rolls; sprinkle with cheese, if desired.

SWEET AND SAVORY BRISKET

makes 4 servings

1 teaspoon salt, divided

½ teaspoon black pepper

1 small beef brisket (2½ to 3 pounds), trimmed

1 large onion, thinly sliced

½ cup beef or chicken broth

⅓ cup chili sauce

1 tablespoon packed brown sugar

½ teaspoon dried thyme

¼ teaspoon ground cinnamon

2 large sweet potatoes, peeled and cut into 1-inch pieces

1 cup pitted prunes

¼ cup water

2 tablespoons cornstarch

1. Rub ½ teaspoon salt and pepper into all sides of beef. Place beef in Instant Pot; top with onion. Combine broth, chili sauce, brown sugar, thyme, cinnamon and remaining ½ teaspoon salt in small bowl; mix well. Pour over beef and onion.

2. Secure lid and move pressure release valve to Sealing position. Press Pressure Cook or Manual; cook at high pressure 70 minutes.

3. When cooking is complete, use natural release for 10 minutes, then release remaining pressure. Remove beef to cutting board; tent with foil.

4. Add sweet potatoes and prunes to pot. Secure lid and move pressure release valve to Sealing position. Press Pressure Cook or Manual; cook at high pressure 3 minutes. When cooking is complete, use quick release. Remove vegetables to bowl with slotted spoon.

5. Stir water into cornstarch in small bowl until smooth. Press Sauté; add cornstarch mixture to pot. Cook and stir 1 to 2 minutes or until sauce thickens.

6. Cut brisket into thin slices across the grain. Serve with sweet potato mixture and sauce.

MEAT LOAF

makes 6 servings

1 tablespoon olive oil

1 small onion, finely chopped

½ red bell pepper, finely chopped

3 cloves garlic, minced

1 teaspoon dried oregano

1½ cups water

2 pounds ground meat loaf mix or 1 pound *each* ground beef and ground pork

1 egg

3 tablespoons tomato paste

1 teaspoon salt

½ teaspoon black pepper

1. Press Sauté; heat oil in Instant Pot. Add onion, bell pepper, garlic and oregano; cook and stir 3 minutes or until vegetables are softened. Remove to large bowl; let cool 5 minutes. Wipe out pot with paper towels; add water and rack to pot.

2. Add meat loaf mix, egg, tomato paste, salt and black pepper to vegetable mixture; mix well. Tear off 18×12-inch piece of foil; fold in half crosswise to create 12×9-inch rectangle. Shape meat mixture into 7×5-inch oval on foil; bring up sides of foil to create pan, leaving top of meat loaf uncovered. Place foil with meat loaf on rack in pot.

3. Secure lid and move pressure release valve to Sealing position. Press Pressure Cook or Manual; cook at high pressure 37 minutes.

4. When cooking is complete, use quick release. Remove meat loaf to cutting board; tent with foil. Let stand 10 minutes before slicing.

TEX-MEX CHILI

makes 4 to 6 servings

4 slices bacon, chopped

⅓ cup all-purpose flour

1½ teaspoons salt, divided

¼ teaspoon black pepper

2 pounds boneless beef top round or chuck shoulder steak, cut into ½-inch pieces

1 medium onion, chopped, plus additional for garnish

2 cloves garlic, minced

1¼ cups water

¼ cup chili powder

1 teaspoon dried oregano

1 teaspoon ground cumin

½ to 1 teaspoon ground red pepper

½ teaspoon hot pepper sauce

1. Press Sauté; cook bacon in Instant Pot until crisp. Remove to paper towel-lined plate.

2. Combine flour, ½ teaspoon salt and black pepper in large resealable food storage bag. Add beef; toss to coat. Add beef to bacon drippings in two batches; cook about 5 minutes or until browned. Remove to plate.

3. Add onion to pot; cook and stir 3 minutes or until softened. Add garlic; cook and stir 1 minute. Return beef and bacon to pot. Add water, chili powder, remaining 1 teaspoon salt, oregano, cumin, red pepper and hot pepper sauce; cook and stir 2 minutes, scraping up browned bits from bottom of pot.

4. Secure lid and move pressure release valve to Sealing position. Press Pressure Cook or Manual; cook at high pressure 20 minutes.

5. When cooking is complete, use natural release for 10 minutes, then release remaining pressure. Garnish with additional onion.

TIP: Texas chili doesn't contain any beans. But if you want to stretch this recipe and dilute some of the spiciness—and you don't live in Texas!—you can add canned pinto beans to the chili after the pressure has been released. Press Sauté and cook until the beans are heated through.

ITALIAN BEEF SANDWICHES

makes 4 servings

1 jar (16 ounces) sliced pepperoncini

1 jar (16 ounces) giardiniera

2 to 2½ pounds boneless beef chuck roast

½ cup beef broth

1 tablespoon Italian seasoning

4 French or sub rolls, split

1. Drain pepperoncini, reserving ½ cup liquid. Set aside ½ cup pepperoncini for sandwiches. Drain giardiniera, reserving ½ cup vegetables for sandwiches.

2. Combine beef, remaining pepperoncini and reserved ½ cup pepperoncini liquid, remaining giardiniera vegetables, broth and Italian seasoning in Instant Pot.

3. Secure lid and move pressure release valve to Sealing position. Press Pressure Cook or Manual; cook at high pressure 60 minutes.

4. When cooking is complete, use natural release for 15 minutes, then release remaining pressure. Remove beef to large bowl; let stand until cool enough to handle. Shred beef into bite-size pieces. Add ½ cup cooking liquid; toss to coat.

5. Fill rolls with beef, reserved pepperoncini and reserved giardiniera vegetables. Serve with warm cooking liquid for dipping.

Instant Pot

BEEF

CORNED BEEF AND CABBAGE

makes 3 to 4 servings

1 **corned beef brisket (3 to 4 pounds) with seasoning packet**

2 **cups water**

1 **head cabbage (about 1½ pounds), cut into 6 wedges**

1 **package (16 ounces) baby carrots**

1. Place corned beef in Instant Pot, fat side up; sprinkle with seasoning. Pour water into pot.

2. Secure lid and move pressure release valve to Sealing position. Press Pressure Cook or Manual; cook at high pressure 90 minutes.

3. When cooking is complete, use natural release for 10 minutes, then release remaining pressure. Remove beef to cutting board; tent with foil.

4. Add cabbage and carrots to pot. Secure lid and move pressure release valve to Sealing position. Press Pressure Cook or Manual; cook at high pressure 4 minutes. When cooking is complete, use quick release.

5. Slice corned beef; serve with vegetables.

SOUTHWESTERN CHILE BEEF

makes 4 servings

2 tablespoons vegetable oil

2 pounds beef round roast, cut into bite-size pieces

1 onion, finely chopped

2 cloves garlic, minced

1 teaspoon all-purpose flour

1 teaspoon salt

1 teaspoon dried oregano

½ teaspoon ground cumin

¼ teaspoon black pepper

5 canned whole green chiles, chopped

1 canned chipotle pepper in adobo sauce, chopped

Hot cooked polenta, rice or pasta (optional)

1. Press Sauté; heat 1 tablespoon oil in Instant Pot. Add half of beef; cook about 5 minutes or until browned, stirring occasionally. Remove to plate. Add remaining oil and beef; cook 3 minutes, stirring occasionally. Add onion and garlic; cook and stir 3 minutes or until beef is browned and onion is softened. Return first half of beef to pot. Add flour, salt, oregano, cumin and black pepper; cook and stir 30 seconds. Stir in green chiles and chipotle pepper; mix well.

2. Secure lid and move pressure release valve to Sealing position. Press Pressure Cook or Manual; cook at high pressure 35 minutes.

3. When cooking is complete, use natural release for 5 minutes, then release remaining pressure.

4. Press Sauté; cook 5 to 10 minutes or until sauce is reduced and thickens slightly. Serve over polenta, if desired.

BEEF FAJITA SOUP

makes 8 servings

1 pound beef stew meat, cut into 1-inch pieces

1 can (about 15 ounces) pinto beans, rinsed and drained

1 can (about 15 ounces) black beans, rinsed and drained

1 can (about 14 ounces) beef broth

1 can (about 10 ounces) diced tomatoes with green chiles

1 green bell pepper, cut into ½-inch slices

1 red bell pepper, cut into ½-inch slices

1 onion, cut into ¼-inch slices

2 teaspoons ground cumin

1 teaspoon seasoned salt

½ teaspoon black pepper

Optional toppings: sour cream, shredded Monterey Jack or Cheddar cheese, chopped olives

1. Combine beef, beans, broth, tomatoes, bell peppers, onion, cumin, seasoned salt and black pepper in Instant Pot; mix well.

2. Secure lid and move pressure release valve to Sealing position. Press Pressure Cook or Manual; cook at high pressure 25 minutes.

3. When cooking is complete, use natural release for 10 minutes, then release remaining pressure. Serve with desired toppings.

Instant Pot

PORK

PERFECT BBQ RIBS

1 rack pork baby back ribs (about 3 pounds)

1/3 cup barbecue seasoning or grilling rub

2 cups apple juice

1/4 cup cider vinegar

1 tablespoon liquid smoke

1 cup barbecue sauce, plus additional for serving

1. Remove membrane covering bones on underside of ribs. Rub barbecue seasoning generously over both sides of ribs, pressing to adhere.

2. Combine apple juice, vinegar and liquid smoke in Instant Pot; mix well. Stand ribs vertically in liquid, coiling ribs into a ring to fit in pot.

3. Secure lid and move pressure release valve to Sealing position. Press Pressure Cook or Manual; cook at high pressure 20 minutes. Preheat broiler. Line baking sheet with foil.

4. When cooking is complete, use natural release for 5 minutes, then release remaining pressure. Remove ribs to prepared baking sheet, meaty side up. Brush both sides of ribs with 1 cup barbecue sauce.

5. Broil about 5 minutes or until sauce begins to bubble and char. Cut into individual ribs; serve with additional sauce.

Instant Pot

PORK

CHILI—SPICED PORK LOIN

makes 4 servings

1 boneless pork loin roast
   (2 to 2½ pounds),
   trimmed

1¼ cups orange juice,
   divided

1 cup chopped onion

2 cloves garlic, minced

1 tablespoon cider vinegar

1½ teaspoons chili powder

1 teaspoon salt

¼ teaspoon dried thyme

¼ teaspoon ground cumin

¼ teaspoon ground
   cinnamon

⅛ teaspoon ground allspice

⅛ teaspoon ground cloves

2 tablespoons olive oil

   Fruit Chutney (recipe
   follows, optional)

1. Place pork in large resealable food storage bag or glass dish. Combine ½ cup orange juice, onion, garlic, vinegar, chili powder, salt, thyme, cumin, cinnamon, allspice and cloves in small bowl; mix well. Pour marinade over pork; seal bag and turn to coat. Refrigerate 2 to 4 hours or overnight.

2. Remove pork from marinade; reserve marinade. Press Sauté; heat oil in Instant Pot. Add pork; cook about 6 minutes or until browned on all sides. Stir in remaining ¾ cup orange juice and reserved marinade, scraping up browned bits from bottom of pot.

3. Secure lid and move pressure release valve to Sealing position. Press Pressure Cook or Manual; cook at high pressure 20 minutes.

4. When cooking is complete, use natural release for 10 minutes, then release remaining pressure. Remove pork to cutting board; tent with foil. Let stand 10 minutes before slicing.

5. Meanwhile, prepare Fruit Chutney, if desired. Or press Sauté; cook until liquid in pot is reduced by one third. Serve with pork.

FRUIT CHUTNEY: Add ¼ cup apricot preserves or orange marmalade to cooking liquid after removing pork from pot. Press Sauté; cook 10 minutes, stirring occasionally. Add 1 diced mango, ½ cup diced fresh pineapple, 2 minced green onions and 1 tablespoon minced jalapeño pepper; cook and stir 5 minutes. Serve with pork.

PORK PICADILLO

makes 4 servings

1 tablespoon olive oil

1 pound boneless pork country-style ribs, trimmed and cut into 1/2-inch pieces

1 onion, chopped

2 cloves garlic, minced

1 can (about 14 ounces) diced tomatoes

1/2 cup raisins

2 tablespoons cider vinegar

2 canned chipotle peppers in adobo sauce, chopped

1/2 teaspoon salt

1/2 teaspoon ground cumin

1/2 teaspoon ground cinnamon

1. Press Sauté; heat oil in Instant Pot. Add pork; cook about 6 minutes or until browned, stirring occasionally. Add onion; cook and stir 2 minutes. Add garlic; cook and stir 30 seconds. Stir in tomatoes, raisins, vinegar, chipotle peppers, salt, cumin and cinnamon, scraping up browned bits from bottom of pot.

2. Secure lid and move pressure release valve to Sealing position. Press Pressure Cook or Manual; cook at high pressure 25 minutes.

3. When cooking is complete, use natural release for 10 minutes, then release remaining pressure. Stir pork mixture with tongs, breaking up pork into smaller pieces.

CHORIZO BURRITOS

makes 4 servings

14 ounces uncooked Mexican chorizo sausages, cut into bite-size pieces

2 green or red bell peppers, cut into 1-inch pieces

1 can (about 15 ounces) kidney or pinto beans, rinsed and drained

1 can (about 14 ounces) diced tomatoes

1 can (11 ounces) corn, drained

$\frac{1}{2}$ teaspoon ground cumin

$\frac{1}{2}$ teaspoon ground cinnamon

8 (8-inch) flour tortillas, warmed

2 cups hot cooked rice

1 cup (4 ounces) shredded Monterey Jack cheese

1. Combine chorizo, bell peppers, beans, tomatoes, corn, cumin and cinnamon in Instant Pot; mix well.

2. Secure lid and move pressure release valve to Sealing position. Press Pressure Cook or Manual; cook at high pressure 10 minutes.

3. When cooking is complete, use natural release for 10 minutes, then release remaining pressure.

4. Press Sauté; cook about 5 minutes or until chorizo mixture thickens, stirring occasionally.

5. Spoon chorizo mixture down centers of tortillas; top with rice and cheese. Roll up tortillas; serve immediately.

CHILI VERDE

makes 4 servings

1 tablespoon vegetable oil

1 pound boneless pork loin, cut into 1-inch pieces

1 onion, cut in half and thinly sliced

1 pound tomatillos, husks removed, rinsed and coarsely chopped

6 cloves garlic, minced

1 teaspoon ground cumin

1 can (about 15 ounces) Great Northern beans, rinsed and drained

1 can (4 ounces) diced green chiles

1 teaspoon salt

¼ teaspoon black pepper

¼ cup chopped fresh cilantro

1. Press Sauté; heat oil in Instant Pot. Add pork; cook about 6 minutes or until browned, stirring occasionally. Remove to plate.

2. Add onion to pot; cook and stir 3 minutes or until softened. Add tomatillos, garlic and cumin; cook and stir 3 minutes, scraping up browned bits from bottom of pot. Stir in beans, chiles, salt, pepper and pork; mix well.

3. Secure lid and move pressure release valve to Sealing position. Press Pressure Cook or Manual; cook at high pressure 8 minutes.

4. When cooking is complete, use natural release for 10 minutes, then release remaining pressure. Stir in cilantro.

Instant Pot

PORK

PULLED PORK SANDWICHES

makes 6 to 8 servings

2 tablespoons coarse salt

2 tablespoons packed brown sugar

2 tablespoons paprika

1 teaspoon dry mustard

1 teaspoon black pepper

1 boneless pork shoulder roast (about 3 pounds), cut into 3-inch pieces

1 cup ketchup

⅓ cup cider vinegar

6 to 8 large Kaiser or sandwich rolls, split

¾ cup barbecue sauce

1. Combine salt, brown sugar, paprika, mustard and pepper in small bowl; mix well. Rub mixture over all sides of pork.

2. Combine ketchup and vinegar in pot; mix well. Place pork pieces in sauce; do not stir.

3. Secure lid and move pressure release valve to sealing position. Press Pressure Cook or Manual; cook at high pressure 60 minutes.

4. When cooking is complete, use natural release for 10 minutes, then release remaining pressure. Remove pork to large bowl or plate; let stand until cool enough to handle.

5. Shred pork into bite-size pieces. Add ½ cup cooking liquid, if desired; toss to coat. Serve on rolls with barbecue sauce.

HONEY GINGER RIBS

makes 4 servings

2 pounds pork baby back ribs, trimmed and cut into 2-rib sections

4 green onions, chopped

½ cup hoisin sauce, divided

3 tablespoons dry sherry or rice wine

2 tablespoons honey

2 tablespoons soy sauce

1 tablespoon cider vinegar

1 tablespoon packed brown sugar

2 cloves garlic, minced

1 teaspoon minced fresh ginger

¼ teaspoon Chinese five-spice powder

⅓ cup chicken or beef broth

2 tablespoons cornstarch

Sesame seeds (optional)

1. Place ribs in large resealable food storage bag. Combine green onions, ¼ cup hoisin sauce, sherry, honey, soy sauce, vinegar, brown sugar, garlic, ginger and five-spice powder in medium bowl; mix well. Pour marinade over ribs. Seal bag; turn to coat. Refrigerate 2 to 4 hours or overnight, turning occasionally.

2. Pour broth into Instant Pot; add ribs and marinade. Secure lid and move pressure release valve to Sealing position. Press Pressure Cook or Manual; cook at high pressure 25 minutes.

3. When cooking is complete, use natural release for 10 minutes, then release remaining pressure. Remove ribs to plate; tent with foil.

4. Skim excess fat from surface of sauce. Place cornstarch in small bowl; stir in 2 tablespoons sauce until smooth. Press Sauté; add cornstarch mixture to pot, stirring constantly. Cook and stir about 2 minutes or until sauce thickens slightly. Add remaining ¼ cup hoisin sauce; cook and stir until heated through.

5. Brush sauce over ribs before serving. Sprinkle with sesame seeds, if desired.

Instant Pot

PORK

CIDER PORK AND ONIONS

makes 8 servings

1 tablespoon vegetable oil

1 bone-in pork shoulder
   roast (3½ to 4 pounds)

4 onions, cut into ¼-inch
   slices (about 4 cups)

1 cup apple cider, divided

1 teaspoon salt, divided

4 cloves garlic, minced

1 teaspoon dried rosemary

½ teaspoon black pepper

1. Press Sauté; heat oil in Instant Pot. Add pork; cook until browned on all sides. Remove to plate. Add onions, ¼ cup cider and ½ teaspoon salt to pot; cook 8 minutes or until onions are softened, scraping up browned bits from bottom of pot. Add garlic and rosemary, cook and stir 1 minute. Return pork to pot; sprinkle with remaining ½ teaspoon salt and pepper. Pour remaining ¾ cup cider over pork.

2. Secure lid and move pressure release valve to Sealing position. Press Pressure Cook or Manual; cook at high pressure 75 minutes.

3. When cooking is complete, use natural release. Remove pork to cutting board; tent with foil.

4. Meanwhile, press Sauté; cook 10 to 15 minutes or until sauce is reduced by one third. Skim fat from sauce; season with additional salt and pepper. Cut pork; serve with sauce.

HOT AND SWEET SAUSAGE SANDWICHES

makes 5 servings

1½ cups pasta sauce

1 large sweet onion, cut into ¼-inch slices

1 medium green bell pepper, cut into ½-inch slices

1 medium red bell pepper, cut into ½-inch slices

1½ tablespoons packed dark brown sugar

1 package (16 ounces) hot Italian sausage links (5 sausages)

5 Italian rolls, split

1. Combine pasta sauce, onion, bell peppers and brown sugar in Instant Pot; mix well. Add sausages to pot; spoon some of sauce mixture over sausages.

2. Secure lid and move pressure release valve to Sealing position. Press Pressure Cook or Manual; cook at high pressure 5 minutes.

3. When cooking is complete, use natural release for 10 minutes, then release remaining pressure. Remove sausages to plate; tent with foil.

4. Press Sauté; cook 10 minutes or until sauce is reduced by one third, stirring occasionally. Serve sausages in rolls; top with sauce.

TIP: If you have leftover sauce, refrigerate or freeze it and serve over pasta or polenta. Top with grated Parmesan cheese.

PORK ROAST WITH FRUIT

makes 8 servings

2 cups water

2 tablespoons salt

1 tablespoon sugar

1 teaspoon dried thyme

1 bay leaf

½ teaspoon black pepper

1 boneless pork loin roast (3 to 3½ pounds)

1 tablespoon olive oil

⅓ cup dry red wine

Juice of ½ lemon

2 cloves garlic, minced

2 cups green grapes

1 cup dried apricots

1 cup dried prunes

1. Combine water, salt, sugar, thyme, bay leaf and pepper in large resealable food storage bag. Add pork; seal bag and turn to coat. Refrigerate overnight or up to 2 days, turning occasionally.

2. Remove pork from brine; discard liquid. Pat dry with paper towels. Press Sauté; heat oil in Instant Pot. Add pork; cook about 10 minutes or until browned on all sides. Remove to plate. Add wine, lemon juice and garlic to pot; cook and stir 1 minute, scraping up browned bits from bottom of pot. Add grapes, apricots and prunes; mix well. Return pork to pot.

3. Secure lid and move pressure release valve to Sealing position. Press Pressure Cook or Manual; cook at high pressure 20 minutes.

4. When cooking is complete, use natural release. Remove pork to cutting board; tent with foil and let stand 10 minutes.

5. Meanwhile, press Sauté; cook 10 minutes or until sauce is reduced and thickens slightly. Slice pork; serve with sauce.

JERK PORK AND SWEET POTATO STEW

2 tablespoons all-purpose flour

1 teaspoon salt

1/4 teaspoon black pepper

1¼ pounds boneless pork shoulder, cut into 1-inch pieces

2 tablespoons vegetable oil

4 tablespoons minced green onions, divided

1 small jalapeño pepper,* seeded and minced

1 clove garlic, minced

1/8 teaspoon ground allspice

1 cup chicken broth

1 large sweet potato, peeled and cut into ¾-inch pieces

1 cup thawed frozen corn

1 tablespoon lime juice

Hot cooked rice (optional)

Jalapeño peppers can sting and irritate the skin, so wear rubber gloves when handling and do not touch your eyes.

1. Combine flour, salt and black pepper in large resealable food storage bag. Add pork; toss to coat. Press Sauté; heat oil in Instant Pot. Add pork in two batches, cook about 5 minutes or until browned. Remove to plate.

2. Add 2 tablespoons green onions, jalapeño, garlic and allspice to pot; cook and stir 30 seconds. Stir in broth, scraping up browned bits from bottom of pot. Return pork to pot.

3. Secure lid and move pressure release valve to Sealing position. Press Pressure Cook or Manual; cook at high pressure 18 minutes. When cooking is complete, use quick release.

4. Add sweet potato to pot. Secure lid and move pressure release valve to Sealing position. Press Pressure Cook or Manual; cook at high pressure 2 minutes.

5. When cooking is complete, use quick release. Stir in corn, remaining 2 tablespoons green onions and lime juice; let stand 2 minutes or until corn is heated through. Serve with rice, if desired.

Instant Pot

BEANS & GRAINS

WHITE BEANS AND TOMATOES

1 pound dried cannellini
    beans, soaked
    8 hours or overnight

2 tablespoons olive oil

2 medium onions, chopped

1 tablespoon minced garlic

1 tablespoon tomato paste

4 teaspoons dried oregano

2 teaspoons salt

1 can (28 ounces)
    crushed tomatoes

2 cups water

Black pepper (optional)

1. Drain and rinse beans. Press Sauté; heat oil in Instant Pot. Add onions; cook and stir 5 to 7 minutes or until tender and lightly browned. Add garlic, tomato paste, oregano and salt; cook and stir 1 minute. Stir in beans, tomatoes and water; mix well.

2. Secure lid and move pressure release valve to Sealing position. Press Pressure Cook or Manual; cook at high pressure 16 minutes.

3. When cooking is complete, use natural release for 10 minutes, then release remaining pressure. Season with black pepper, if desired.

CHEESY POLENTA

makes 6 servings

5 cups vegetable broth

½ teaspoon salt

1½ cups uncooked instant polenta

½ cup grated Parmesan cheese

¼ cup (½ stick) butter, cubed, plus additional for serving

Fried sage leaves (optional)

1. Combine broth and salt in Instant Pot; slowly whisk in polenta until blended.

2. Secure lid and move pressure release valve to Sealing position. Press Pressure Cook or Manual; cook at high pressure 5 minutes.

3. When cooking is complete, use natural release for 5 minutes, then release remaining pressure.

4. Whisk in cheese and ¼ cup butter until well blended. (Polenta may appear separated immediately after cooking but will come together when stirred.) Serve with additional butter; garnish with sage.

TIP: Spread any leftover polenta in a baking dish and refrigerate until cold. Cut the cold polenta into sticks or slices, brush with olive oil and pan-fry or grill until lightly browned.

NOTE: Chicken broth may be substituted for vegetable broth. Or use water and add an additional ½ teaspoon salt when whisking in the polenta.

FARRO RISOTTO WITH MUSHROOMS AND SPINACH

makes 4 servings

2 tablespoons olive oil, divided

1 onion, chopped

12 ounces cremini mushrooms, trimmed and quartered

1 teaspoon salt

1/4 teaspoon black pepper

2 cloves garlic, minced

1 cup uncooked pearled farro

1 sprig fresh thyme

1 1/2 cups vegetable broth

1 package (5 to 6 ounces) baby spinach

1/2 cup grated Parmesan cheese

1. Press Sauté; heat 1 tablespoon oil in Instant Pot. Add onion; cook and stir 5 minutes or until translucent. Add remaining 1 tablespoon oil, mushrooms, salt and pepper; cook about 8 minutes or until mushrooms have released their liquid and are browned, stirring occasionally. Add garlic; cook and stir 1 minute. Add farro and thyme; cook and stir 1 minute. Stir in broth; mix well.

2. Secure lid and move pressure release valve to Sealing position. Press Pressure Cook or Manual; cook at high pressure 10 minutes.

3. When cooking is complete, use natural release for 10 minutes, then release remaining pressure. Remove and discard thyme sprig.

4. Add spinach and cheese; stir until spinach is wilted.

SWEET POTATO
AND BLACK BEAN CHILI

makes 6 servings

1 tablespoon olive oil

1 large onion, chopped

4 teaspoons chili powder

2 cloves garlic, minced

1 teaspoon salt

1 teaspoon chipotle
chili powder

½ teaspoon ground cumin

2 cans (about 15 ounces
each) black beans,
rinsed and drained

1 large sweet potato,
peeled and cut
into ½-inch pieces

1 can (about 14 ounces)
diced tomatoes

1 can (about 14 ounces)
crushed tomatoes

1½ cups vegetable broth
or water

Optional toppings:
sour cream, sliced
green onions, shredded
Cheddar cheese and
tortilla strips

1. Press Sauté; heat oil in Instant Pot. Add onion; cook and stir 3 minutes or until softened. Add chili powder, garlic, salt, chipotle chili powder and cumin; cook and stir 1 minute. Add beans, sweet potato, diced tomatoes, crushed tomatoes and broth; mix well.

2. Secure lid and move pressure release valve to Sealing position. Press Pressure Cook or Manual; cook at high pressure 4 minutes.

3. When cooking is complete, use quick release.

4. Press Sauté; cook and stir 3 to 5 minutes or until chili thickens slightly. Serve with desired toppings.

BARLEY WITH CURRANTS AND PINE NUTS

makes 4 to 6 servings

2 tablespoons butter

1 onion, finely chopped

2 cups vegetable broth

1 cup uncooked pearl barley

½ cup currants

½ teaspoon salt

¼ teaspoon black pepper

½ cup pine nuts, toasted*

To toast pine nuts, cook in small skillet over medium heat 3 minutes or until lightly browned, stirring frequently.

1. Press Sauté; melt butter in Instant Pot. Add onion; cook and stir 5 minutes or until tender. Stir in broth, barley, currants, salt and pepper; mix well.

2. Secure lid and move pressure release valve to Sealing position. Press Pressure Cook or Manual; cook at high pressure 18 minutes.

3. When cooking is complete, use natural release for 10 minutes, then release remaining pressure.

4. Stir in pine nuts. Serve warm or at room temperature.

GREEK RICE

2 tablespoons butter

1¾ cups uncooked long grain rice, rinsed well and drained

1¾ cups vegetable or chicken broth

1 teaspoon Greek seasoning

1 teaspoon dried oregano

¼ teaspoon salt

1 cup pitted kalamata olives, drained and chopped

¾ cup chopped roasted red peppers

Crumbled feta cheese (optional)

Chopped fresh Italian parsley (optional)

1. Press Sauté; melt butter in Instant Pot. Add rice; cook 5 to 6 minutes or until golden brown, stirring occasionally. Add broth, Greek seasoning, oregano and salt; mix well.

2. Secure lid and move pressure release valve to Sealing position. Press Pressure Cook or Manual; cook at high pressure 4 minutes.

3. When cooking is complete, use natural release for 10 minutes, then release remaining pressure.

4. Stir in olives and roasted peppers; garnish with cheese and parsley.

BULGUR PILAF WITH CARAMELIZED ONIONS AND KALE

makes 4 servings

- 1 tablespoon olive oil
- 1 medium onion, cut into thin wedges
- 1 clove garlic, minced
- 2 cups chopped kale
- 2¾ cups vegetable or chicken broth
- 1 cup medium grain bulgur
- 1 teaspoon salt
- ¼ teaspoon black pepper

1. Press Sauté; heat oil in Instant Pot. Add onion; cook about 10 minutes or until golden brown, stirring frequently. Add garlic; cook and stir 1 minute. Add kale; cook and stir about 1 minute or until wilted. Stir in broth, bulgur, salt and pepper; mix well.

2. Secure lid and move pressure release valve to Sealing position. Press Pressure Cook or Manual; cook at high pressure 8 minutes.

3. When cooking is complete, use natural release for 5 minutes, then release remaining pressure.

SHORTCUT BAKED BEANS

makes 6 to 8 servings

5 slices thick-cut bacon, chopped

1 small onion, chopped

3½ cups water

1 pound dried pinto beans, rinsed and sorted

1 cup barbecue sauce

¼ cup ketchup

½ teaspoon salt

1. Press Sauté; cook bacon in Instant Pot until crisp. Drain off all but 1 tablespoon drippings.

2. Add onion to pot; cook and stir 3 minutes or until softened. Add water and beans; cook 1 minute, scraping up browned bits from bottom of pot. Stir in barbecue sauce and ketchup; mix well.

3. Secure lid and move pressure release valve to Sealing position. Press Pressure Cook or Manual; cook at high pressure 50 minutes.

4. When cooking is complete, use natural release for 15 minutes, then release remaining pressure. Stir beans; season with salt. If there is excess liquid in pot, press Sauté and cook 3 to 5 minutes or until liquid is reduced, stirring frequently.

ASPARAGUS RISOTTO

makes 4 to 6 servings

4 tablespoons (½ stick) butter, divided

1 tablespoon olive oil

1 onion, finely chopped

1½ cups uncooked arborio rice

1 teaspoon salt

¼ cup dry white wine

4 cups vegetable broth

2½ cups fresh asparagus pieces (about 1 inch)

⅔ cup frozen peas

1 cup grated Parmesan cheese

Shaved Parmesan cheese (optional)

1. Press Sauté; heat 3 tablespoons butter and oil in Instant Pot. Add onion; cook and stir 2 minutes or until softened. Add rice; cook and stir 2 minutes or until rice is translucent. Stir in salt. Add wine; cook and stir about 1 minute or until evaporated. Add broth; mix well.

2. Secure lid and move pressure release valve to Sealing position. Press Pressure Cook or Manual; cook at high pressure 5 minutes.

3. When cooking is complete, use quick release. Stir in asparagus and peas. Secure lid and move pressure release valve to Sealing position. Press Pressure Cook or Manual; cook at high pressure 1 minute.

4. When cooking is complete, use quick release. Stir in remaining 1 tablespoon butter and 1 cup grated cheese. Serve immediately with additional cheese, if desired.

ASPARAGUS-SPINACH RISOTTO: Substitute 1 cup baby spinach or chopped fresh spinach leaves for peas. Proceed as directed.

JALAPEÑO CHEDDAR CORN BREAD

makes 8 servings

1 cup yellow cornmeal

¾ cup all-purpose flour

⅓ cup sugar

2 teaspoons baking powder

1 teaspoon salt

1 cup buttermilk or whole milk

2 eggs

3 tablespoons butter, melted

1 cup (4 ounces) shredded Cheddar cheese

2 jalapeño peppers, seeded and minced* (about ⅓ cup)

1½ cups water

Jalapeño peppers can sting and irritate the skin, so wear rubber gloves when handling peppers and do not touch your eyes.

1. Spray 7-inch springform pan with nonstick cooking spray. Combine cornmeal, flour, sugar, baking powder and salt in large bowl; mix well.

2. Beat buttermilk, eggs and butter in medium bowl until blended. Add to cornmeal mixture; stir just until blended. Stir in cheese and jalapeños until blended. Spread batter evenly in prepared pan; cover with foil.

3. Pour water into Instant Pot; place rack in pot. Place pan on rack. Secure lid and move pressure release valve to Sealing position. Press Pressure Cook or Manual; cook at high pressure 30 minutes.

4. When cooking is complete, use quick release. Remove pan from pot. Uncover; cool on wire rack 5 minutes before serving.

SOUTHWESTERN CORN AND BEANS

makes 6 servings

2 cups dried kidney beans, soaked 8 hours or overnight

1 tablespoon olive oil

1 large onion, chopped

1 jalapeño pepper, minced*

1 clove garlic, minced

2 teaspoons chili powder

½ teaspoon ground cumin

1 can (about 14 ounces) diced tomatoes

1 green bell pepper, cut into 1-inch pieces

½ cup water

1½ teaspoons salt

½ teaspoon black pepper

1 package (16 ounces) frozen corn, thawed

Optional toppings: sour cream, sliced black olives and tortilla chips

*Jalapeño peppers can sting and irritate the skin, so wear rubber gloves when handling peppers and do not touch your eyes.

1. Drain and rinse beans. Press Sauté; heat oil in Instant Pot. Add onion; cook and stir 3 minutes or until softened. Add jalapeño, garlic, chili powder and cumin; cook and stir 1 minute. Add tomatoes, bell pepper, water, salt and black pepper; mix well. Stir in beans.

2. Secure lid and move pressure release valve to Sealing position. Press Pressure Cook or Manual; cook at high pressure 25 minutes.

3. When cooking is complete, use natural release for 10 minutes, then release remaining pressure.

4. Press Sauté; stir in corn. Cook about 5 minutes or until mixture has thickened and corn is heated through, stirring occasionally. Serve with sour cream, olives and tortilla chips, if desired.

SPANISH RICE

makes 6 to 8 servings

1 tablespoon olive oil

1 small onion, chopped

2 cloves garlic, minced

2 cups uncooked brown rice, rinsed well and drained

1 can (about 14 ounces) diced tomatoes with green chiles

1 cup plus 2 tablespoons chicken broth or water

1 teaspoon salt

1. Press Sauté; heat oil in Instant Pot. Add onion and garlic; cook and stir 2 minutes. Add rice; cook and stir 2 minutes. Stir in tomatoes, broth and salt; mix well.

2. Secure lid and move pressure release valve to Sealing position. Press Pressure Cook or Manual; cook at high pressure 24 minutes.

3. When cooking is complete, use natural release for 10 minutes, then release remaining pressure. Fluff rice with fork.

CHICKPEA TIKKA MASALA

makes 4 servings

1¼ cups dried chickpeas, soaked 8 hours or overnight

1 tablespoon olive oil

1 onion, chopped

3 cloves garlic, minced

1 tablespoon minced fresh ginger or ginger paste

1 tablespoon garam masala

1½ teaspoons salt

1 teaspoon ground coriander

1 teaspoon ground cumin

¼ teaspoon ground red pepper

1 can (28 ounces) crushed tomatoes

1 can (about 13 ounces) coconut milk

1 package (about 12 ounces) paneer cheese, cut into 1-inch cubes

Hot cooked basmati rice (optional)

Chopped fresh cilantro

1. Drain and rinse chickpeas. Press Sauté; heat oil in Instant Pot. Add onion; cook and stir 5 minutes or until translucent. Add garlic, ginger, garam masala, salt, coriander, cumin and red pepper; cook and stir 1 minute. Stir in chickpeas, tomatoes and coconut milk; mix well.

2. Secure lid and move pressure release valve to Sealing position. Press Pressure Cook or Manual; cook at high pressure 22 minutes.

3. When cooking is complete, use natural release for 10 minutes, then release remaining pressure.

4. Press Sauté; adjust heat to low. Add paneer to pot; stir gently. Cook 5 minutes or until paneer is heated through, stirring occasionally. Serve with rice, if desired; garnish with cilantro.

VARIATION: For a vegan dish, substitute 1 package (about 12 ounces) firm silken tofu, drained and cut into 1-inch cubes, for the paneer.

PUMPKIN RISOTTO

makes 4 servings

2 tablespoons butter

1 tablespoon olive oil

1 onion, finely chopped

2 cloves garlic, minced

1½ cups uncooked arborio rice

1 teaspoon salt

¼ teaspoon ground nutmeg

⅛ teaspoon black pepper

½ cup dry white wine

4 cups vegetable broth

1 can (15 ounces) pure pumpkin

5 fresh sage leaves

½ cup shredded Parmesan cheese, plus additional for serving

¼ cup roasted pumpkin seeds (pepitas)

1. Press Sauté; heat butter and oil in Instant Pot. Add onion and garlic; cook and stir 3 minutes or until softened. Add rice; cook and stir 4 minutes or until rice is translucent. Stir in salt, nutmeg and pepper. Add wine; cook and stir about 1 minute or until evaporated. Stir in broth, pumpkin and sage; mix well.

2. Secure lid and move pressure release valve to Sealing position. Press Pressure Cook or Manual; cook at high pressure 6 minutes.

3. When cooking is complete, use quick release.

4. Press Sauté; adjust heat to low. Cook about 3 minutes or until risotto reaches desired consistency, stirring constantly. Stir in ½ cup cheese until blended. Serve immediately with additional cheese and pumpkin seeds.

FRIJOLES BORRACHOS (DRUNKEN BEANS)

makes 6 to 8 servings

1 pound dried pinto beans,
   soaked 8 hours
   or overnight

6 slices bacon, chopped

1 large onion, chopped

3 jalapeño peppers,*
   seeded and finely
   chopped

1 tablespoon minced garlic

1 tablespoon dried
   oregano

1 cup dark Mexican beer

1 can (about 14 ounces)
   diced tomatoes

1 cup water

¾ teaspoon salt

¼ cup chopped fresh
   cilantro, plus additional
   for garnish

*Jalapeño peppers can sting and
irritate the skin, so wear rubber
gloves when handling peppers
and do not touch your eyes.*

1. Drain and rinse beans. Press Sauté; cook bacon in Instant Pot until crisp. Drain off all but 2 tablespoons drippings. Add onion to pot; cook and stir 4 minutes or until softened and lightly browned. Add jalapeños, garlic and oregano; cook and stir 1 minute. Stir in beer, scraping up browned bits from bottom of pot. Stir in beans, tomatoes, water and salt; mix well.

2. Secure lid and move pressure release valve to Sealing position. Press Pressure Cook or Manual; cook at high pressure 22 minutes.

3. When cooking is complete, use natural release for 10 minutes, then release remaining pressure.

4. Press Sauté; cook 3 minutes, mashing beans slightly until broth is thickened and creamy. Stir in ¼ cup cilantro until blended; garnish with additional cilantro.

Instant Pot

PASTA

ASIAN CHICKEN AND NOODLES

1 tablespoon vegetable oil

1 pound boneless skinless chicken breasts, cut into 1×½-inch pieces

1 bottle or jar (about 12 ounces) stir-fry sauce

¾ cup chicken broth or water

8 ounces uncooked thin Pad Thai rice noodles (⅛ inch wide)

1 package (16 ounces) frozen stir-fry vegetable blend (do not thaw)

1. Press Sauté; heat oil in Instant Pot. Add chicken; cook about 4 minutes or until no longer pink, stirring frequently.

2. Stir in stir-fry sauce and broth; mix well. Top with noodles, breaking to fit as necessary. Cover with vegetables in even layer. (Do not stir.)

3. Secure lid and move pressure release valve to Sealing position. Press Pressure Cook or Manual; cook at high pressure 2 minutes.

4. When cooking is complete, use quick release. Stir with tongs to separate noodles and coat noodles and vegetables with sauce. If there is excess liquid in pot, press Sauté; cook and stir 2 minutes or until liquid has evaporated.

Instant Pot

PASTA

EASY CHEESY LASAGNA

makes 4 to 6 servings

1 cup ricotta cheese

1¾ cups (7 ounces) shredded Italian blend cheese, divided

1 egg

2 cups pasta sauce

8 no-boil lasagna noodles (about 5 ounces)

1½ cups water

1. Spray 7-inch springform pan with nonstick cooking spray. Beat ricotta, ½ cup shredded cheese and egg in small bowl until well blended.

2. Spread ½ cup pasta sauce on bottom of prepared pan. Top with 2 noodles, breaking to fit and cover sauce layer. Spread one third of ricotta mixture over sauce; top with ¼ cup shredded cheese. Repeat layers of sauce, noodles, ricotta mixture and shredded cheese twice, pressing down gently. Top with remaining 2 noodles, ½ cup pasta sauce and ½ cup shredded cheese. Cover pan with foil sprayed with nonstick cooking spray (or use nonstick foil).

3. Pour water into Instant Pot; place rack in pot. Place pan on rack.

4. Secure lid and move pressure release valve to Sealing position. Press Pressure Cook or Manual; cook at high pressure 16 minutes. Preheat broiler.

5. When cooking is complete, use natural release for 5 minutes, then release remaining pressure. Remove pan from pot. Uncover; place lasagna on baking sheet. Broil about 3 minutes or until top is golden brown in spots.

CHILI WAGON WHEEL PASTA

makes 4 servings

1 tablespoon olive oil

1 pound ground turkey or ground beef

1 cup chopped onion

1 green bell pepper, chopped

2 teaspoons salt

2 teaspoons chili powder

½ teaspoon dried oregano

½ teaspoon black pepper

¼ teaspoon ground allspice

1 can (about 14 ounces) diced tomatoes

1 can (8 ounces) tomato sauce

½ cup water

8 ounces uncooked mini wagon wheel pasta

1 cup (4 ounces) shredded Cheddar cheese

1. Press Sauté; heat oil in Instant Pot. Add turkey; cook 5 minutes or until cooked through, stirring frequently. Add onion and bell pepper; cook and stir 3 minutes or until softened. Add salt, chili powder, oregano, black pepper and allspice; cook and stir 30 seconds. Stir in tomatoes, tomato sauce and water; mix well. Stir in pasta.

2. Secure lid and move pressure release valve to Sealing position. Press Pressure Cook or Manual; cook at high pressure 4 minutes.

3. When cooking is complete, use quick release. Stir in cheese.

Instant Pot

PASTA

CLASSIC MACARONI AND CHEESE

makes 4 to 6 servings

2 cups uncooked elbow macaroni

2 cups water

1½ teaspoons salt, divided

1 can (5 ounces) evaporated milk

3 cups (12 ounces) shredded Colby-Jack cheese*

⅛ teaspoon black pepper

Or substitute 6 ounces each shredded Colby and Monterey Jack cheeses.

1. Combine macaroni, water and 1 teaspoon salt in Instant Pot. Secure lid and move pressure release valve to Sealing position. Press Pressure Cook or Manual; cook at high pressure 4 minutes.

2. When cooking is complete, use quick release.

3. Press Sauté; alternately add milk and handfuls of cheese, stirring constantly until cheese is melted and smooth. Stir in remaining ½ teaspoon salt and pepper.

SPICY SAUSAGE AND PENNE PASTA

makes 4 to 6 servings

- 1 pound bulk hot Italian sausage
- 1 cup chopped onion
- 2 cloves garlic, minced
- 2 teaspoons salt
- 1 teaspoon dried oregano
- 1 teaspoon dried basil
- 2 cans (about 14 ounces each) diced tomatoes
- 1½ cups water
- 8 ounces uncooked penne pasta
- 3 cups broccoli florets (from 1 medium head)
- ½ cup shredded Asiago or Romano cheese

1. Press Sauté; crumble sausage into Instant Pot. Add onion; cook 10 minutes or until sausage is cooked through, stirring frequently. Add garlic, salt, oregano and basil; cook and stir 1 minute. Stir in tomatoes, water and pasta; mix well.

2. Secure lid and move pressure release valve to Sealing position. Press Pressure Cook or Manual; cook at high pressure 3 minutes.

3. When cooking is complete, use quick release. Stir in broccoli. Secure lid and move pressure release valve to Sealing position. Press Pressure Cook or Manual; cook at high pressure 0 minutes. (Set cooking time for 0 minutes; Instant Pot will beep as soon as contents reach pressure.)

4. When cooking is complete, use quick release. Stir pasta; sprinkle with cheese.

PASTA E CECI

makes 4 servings

1 cup dried chickpeas, soaked 8 hours or overnight

3 tablespoons olive oil

1 onion, chopped

1 carrot, chopped

2 teaspoons salt

1 clove garlic, minced

1 teaspoon minced fresh rosemary

1 can (28 ounces) whole tomatoes, undrained, crushed with hands or coarsely chopped

2 cups vegetable broth or water

1 bay leaf

$\frac{1}{8}$ teaspoon red pepper flakes

1 cup uncooked orecchiette pasta

Black pepper

Chopped fresh parsley (optional)

1. Drain and rinse chickpeas. Press Sauté; heat oil in Instant Pot. Add onion and carrot; cook and stir 8 minutes or until vegetables are softened. Add salt, garlic and rosemary; cook and stir 1 minute. Add chickpeas, tomatoes with liquid, broth, bay leaf and red pepper flakes; mix well.

2. Secure lid and move pressure release valve to Sealing position. Press Pressure Cook or Manual; cook at high pressure 15 minutes. When cooking is complete, use natural release for 5 minutes, then release remaining pressure.

3. Stir in pasta. Secure lid and move pressure release valve to Sealing position. Press Pressure Cook or Manual; cook at high pressure 6 minutes.

4. When cooking is complete, use quick release. Remove and discard bay leaf. Season with black pepper; garnish with parsley.

TIP: To crush the tomatoes, take them out of the can one at a time and crush them between your fingers over the pot. Or coarsely chop them with a knife.

QUICK SPAGHETTI SUPPER

makes 4 to 6 servings

1 pound lean ground beef

1 medium onion, chopped

1 teaspoon salt

¼ teaspoon black pepper

1 can (about 15 ounces) chili beans in mild sauce

1 can (about 14 ounces) Italian-seasoned diced tomatoes

2 teaspoons chili powder

¼ teaspoon garlic powder

8 ounces uncooked spaghetti

½ cup water

1½ cups (6 ounces) shredded sharp Cheddar cheese, divided

¼ cup sour cream

1. Press Sauté; add beef, onion, salt and pepper to Instant Pot. Cook about 7 minutes or until beef is no longer pink, stirring to break up meat. Drain fat.

2. Stir in beans, tomatoes, chili powder and garlic powder; mix well. Break spaghetti in half; add to pot with water.

3. Secure lid and move pressure release valve to Sealing position. Press Pressure Cook or Manual; cook at high pressure 5 minutes.

4. When cooking is complete, use quick release.

5. Press Sauté; stir in 1 cup cheese and sour cream. Cook and stir 1 minute or until cheese is melted and mixture is well blended. Turn off heat; cover and let stand 3 minutes or until excess liquid is absorbed and pasta is tender. Sprinkle with remaining ½ cup cheese.

Instant Pot

PASTA

PENNE WITH RICOTTA, TOMATOES AND BASIL

makes 4 servings

2 cans (about 14 ounces each) diced tomatoes with basil, garlic and oregano

2½ cups water

3 teaspoons salt, divided

1 package (16 ounces) uncooked penne pasta

1 container (15 ounces) ricotta cheese

⅔ cup chopped fresh basil

¼ cup extra virgin olive oil

1 tablespoon balsamic vinegar

1 clove garlic, minced

¼ teaspoon black pepper

Grated Parmesan cheese

1. Combine tomatoes, water and 2 teaspoons salt in Instant Pot; mix well. Stir in pasta.

2. Secure lid and move pressure release valve to Sealing position. Press Pressure Cook or Manual; cook at high pressure 5 minutes.

3. Meanwhile, combine ricotta, basil, oil, vinegar, garlic, remaining 1 teaspoon salt and pepper in medium bowl; mix well.

4. When cooking is complete, use quick release. Drain any remaining liquid in pot. Add ricotta mixture to pot; stir gently to coat. Sprinkle with Parmesan just before serving.

Instant Pot

PASTA

ONE-POT PASTA WITH SAUSAGE

makes 6 servings

1 tablespoon olive oil

1 pound smoked sausage (about 4 links), cut into ¼-inch slices

1 onion, diced

1 tablespoon tomato paste

2 cloves garlic, minced

1½ teaspoons dried oregano

¼ teaspoon red pepper flakes

1 can (28 ounces) whole tomatoes, undrained, crushed with hands or coarsely chopped

2½ cups water

1½ teaspoons salt

1 package (16 ounces) uncooked cellentani pasta

1½ cups frozen peas

½ cup shredded Parmesan cheese

⅓ cup shredded fresh basil, plus additional for garnish

1. Press Sauté; heat oil in Instant Pot. Add sausage; cook about 7 minutes or until browned, stirring occasionally. Add onion; cook and stir 3 minutes or until softened. Add tomato paste, garlic, oregano and red pepper flakes; cook and stir 1 minute. Add tomatoes with liquid, water and salt; cook 2 minutes, scraping up browned bits from bottom of pot. Stir in pasta; mix well.

2. Secure lid and move pressure release valve to Sealing position. Press Pressure Cook or Manual; cook at high pressure 5 minutes.

3. When cooking is complete, use quick release.

4. Press Sauté; add peas to pot. Cook and stir 2 minutes. Turn off heat; stir in cheese and ⅓ cup basil. Cover and let stand 2 minutes. Garnish with additional basil.

VARIATION: You can substitute 1 pound uncooked Italian sausage (about 4 links) for the smoked sausage. Remove the casings, cut into ½-inch pieces and proceed with the recipe as directed.

Instant Pot

PASTA

LENTIL BOLOGNESE

makes 6 servings

2 tablespoons olive oil

1 onion, chopped

1 carrot, chopped

1 stalk celery, chopped

2 cloves garlic, minced

1 teaspoon salt

½ teaspoon dried oregano

Pinch red pepper flakes

3 tablespoons tomato paste

¼ cup dry white wine

3¼ cups water or vegetable broth

1 can (28 ounces) crushed tomatoes

1 can (about 14 ounces) diced tomatoes

1 cup dried lentils, rinsed and sorted

1 portobello mushroom, gills removed, finely chopped

2 cups uncooked whole wheat rotini pasta

1. Press Sauté; heat oil in Instant Pot. Add onion, carrot and celery; cook and stir 7 minutes or until onion is lightly browned and carrot is softened.

2. Stir in garlic, salt, oregano and red pepper flakes. Add tomato paste; cook and stir 1 minute. Add wine; cook and stir until absorbed. Stir in water, crushed tomatoes, diced tomatoes, lentils and mushroom; mix well.

3. Secure lid and move pressure release valve to Sealing position. Press Pressure Cook or Manual; cook at high pressure 5 minutes. When cooking is complete, use quick release.

4. Stir in pasta. Secure lid and move pressure release valve to Sealing position. Press Pressure Cook or Manual; cook at high pressure 4 minutes. When cooking is complete, use quick release.

INSTANT CHILI MAC

makes 4 servings

1 pound ground beef

1 cup chopped onion

1 clove garlic, minced

1 tablespoon chili powder

½ teaspoon dried oregano

½ teaspoon ground cumin

¼ teaspoon red pepper flakes

2 cups uncooked macaroni

2 cups water

1 can (about 14 ounces) diced tomatoes

1 teaspoon salt

¼ teaspoon black pepper

1. Press Sauté; add beef, onion and garlic to Instant Pot. Cook about 6 minutes or until beef is no longer pink, stirring to break up meat. Add chili powder, oregano, cumin and red pepper flakes; cook and stir 1 minute. Stir in macaroni, water, tomatoes, salt and black pepper; mix well.

2. Secure lid and move pressure release valve to Sealing position. Press Pressure Cook or Manual; cook at high pressure 5 minutes.

3. When cooking is complete, use quick release.

VEGETABLES

WARM POTATO SALAD

makes 6 to 8 servings

- 2 pounds unpeeled fingerling potatoes
- ¾ cup water
- 3 slices thick-cut bacon, cut into ½-inch pieces
- 1 small onion, diced
- 2 tablespoons olive oil
- ¼ cup cider vinegar
- 2 tablespoons capers, drained
- 1 tablespoon Dijon mustard
- ¾ teaspoon salt
- ¼ teaspoon black pepper
- ⅓ cup chopped fresh parsley

1. Combine potatoes and water in Instant Pot. Secure lid and move pressure release valve to Sealing position. Press Pressure Cook or Manual; cook at high pressure 4 minutes.

2. When cooking is complete, use quick release. Drain potatoes; let stand until cool enough to handle. Dry out pot with paper towel.

3. Press Sauté; cook bacon in pot until crisp. Drain on paper towel-lined plate. Drain off all but 1 tablespoon drippings. Adjust heat to low. Add onion and oil to pot; cook about 10 minutes or until onion begins to turn golden, stirring occasionally. Meanwhile, cut potatoes crosswise into ½-inch slices.

4. Add vinegar, capers, mustard, salt and pepper to pot; mix well. Turn off heat; stir in potatoes. Add parsley and bacon; stir gently to coat.

SHAKSHUKA

makes 4 servings

2 tablespoons extra virgin olive oil

1 large red bell pepper, chopped

1 medium onion, chopped

3 cloves garlic, minced

2 teaspoons sugar

2 teaspoons ground cumin

1 teaspoon paprika

1 teaspoon chili powder

½ teaspoon salt

¼ teaspoon red pepper flakes

1 can (28 ounces) crushed tomatoes

¾ cup (3 ounces) crumbled feta cheese

4 eggs

1. Press Sauté; heat oil in Instant Pot. Add bell pepper and onion; cook and stir 3 minutes or until vegetables are softened. Add garlic, sugar, cumin, paprika, chili powder, salt and red pepper flakes; cook and stir 1 minute. Stir in tomatoes; mix well.

2. Secure lid and move pressure release valve to Sealing position. Press Pressure Cook or Manual; cook at high pressure 10 minutes.

3. When cooking is complete, use quick release.

4. Stir in cheese. Make four wells in sauce for eggs, leaving space between each. Slide eggs, one at a time, into wells in sauce. (For best results, crack each egg into small bowl before sliding into sauce.)

5. Secure lid and move pressure release valve to Sealing position. Cook at low pressure 1 minute. When cooking is complete, use quick release. To cook eggs longer, press Sauté and cook until desired doneness.

MASHED SWEET POTATOES AND PARSNIPS

makes 6 servings

- 2 large sweet potatoes (about 1½ pounds), peeled and cut into 1-inch pieces
- 2 medium parsnips (about 12 ounces), peeled and cut into ½-inch slices
- ½ cup water
- 1 teaspoon salt
- ¼ cup evaporated milk
- 2 tablespoons butter
- ⅛ teaspoon ground nutmeg
- ¼ cup chopped fresh chives or green onions

1. Combine sweet potatoes, parsnips, water and salt in Instant Pot. Secure lid and move pressure release valve to Sealing position. Press Pressure Cook or Manual; cook at high pressure 10 minutes.

2. When cooking is complete, use quick release.

3. Add milk, butter and nutmeg to pot; mash with potato masher until smooth. Stir in chives.

SWEET AND SOUR RED CABBAGE

makes 8 servings

2 slices thick-cut bacon, chopped

1 cup chopped onion

1 head red cabbage (2 to 3 pounds), thinly sliced (about 8 cups)

1 pound unpeeled Granny Smith apples, cut into ½-inch pieces (about 2 medium)

½ cup honey

½ cup cider vinegar

¼ cup plus 3 tablespoons water, divided

1 teaspoon salt

1 teaspoon celery salt

¼ teaspoon black pepper

2 tablespoons all-purpose flour

1. Press Sauté, cook bacon in Instant Pot until crisp. Remove to paper towel-lined plate.

2. Add onion to pot; cook and stir 3 minutes or until softened. Stir in cabbage, apples, honey, vinegar, ¼ cup water, salt, celery salt and pepper; mix well.

3. Secure lid and move pressure release valve to Sealing position. Press Pressure Cook or Manual; cook at high pressure 5 minutes.

4. When cooking is complete, use natural release for 10 minutes, then release remaining pressure.

5. Stir remaining 3 tablespoons water into flour in small bowl until smooth. Press Sauté; add flour mixture to pot. Cook and stir about 3 minutes or until sauce thickens. Sprinkle with bacon; serve warm.

GARLIC PARMESAN SPAGHETTI SQUASH

makes 2 servings

1 medium spaghetti squash (2 to 2½ pounds)

1 cup water

2 tablespoons extra virgin olive oil

1 clove garlic, minced

¼ teaspoon salt

¼ teaspoon red pepper flakes

⅛ teaspoon black pepper

½ cup shredded Parmesan cheese

⅓ cup chopped fresh parsley

1. Cut squash in half; remove and discard seeds. Pour water into Instant Pot; place rack in pot. Place squash halves on rack, cut sides up.

2. Secure lid and move pressure release valve to sealing or locked position. Cook at high pressure 7 minutes.

3. When cooking is complete, use quick release. Remove squash to plate; let stand until cool enough to handle. Use fork to shred squash into long strands, reserving shells for serving, if desired.

4. Pour out cooking water and dry pot with paper towel. Press Sauté; adjust heat to low. Add oil, garlic, salt, red pepper flakes and black pepper to pot; cook and stir 2 to 3 minutes or until garlic begins to turn golden. Turn off heat. Add squash, cheese and parsley; stir gently just until blended. Serve immediately.

SPICY ASIAN GREEN BEANS

makes 4 servings

1 cup water

1 pound fresh green beans, trimmed

2 tablespoons chopped green onions

2 tablespoons dry sherry or chicken broth

1½ tablespoons reduced-sodium soy sauce

1 teaspoon chili sauce with garlic

1 teaspoon dark sesame oil

1 clove garlic, minced

1. Pour water into Instant Pot; place rack in pot. Place beans on rack. (Arrange beans perpendicular to rack to prevent beans from falling through.)

2. Secure lid and move pressure release valve to Sealing position. Press Pressure Cook or Manual; cook at high pressure 2 minutes.

3. When cooking is complete, use quick release. Remove rack from pot; drain off and discard cooking liquid. Place beans in large bowl.

4. Press Sauté; add green onions, sherry, soy sauce, chili sauce, oil and garlic to pot. Cook and stir 1 to 2 minutes or until heated through.

5. Pour sauce over beans; toss to coat.

CHUNKY RANCH POTATOES

3 pounds unpeeled red
   potatoes, quartered

½ cup water

1 teaspoon salt

½ cup ranch dressing

½ cup grated Parmesan
   cheese

¼ cup minced fresh chives

1. Combine potatoes, water and salt in Instant Pot; mix well.

2. Secure lid and move pressure release valve to Sealing position. Press Pressure Cook or Manual; cook at high pressure 5 minutes.

3. When cooking is complete, use quick release.

4. Add ranch dressing, cheese and chives to pot; stir gently to coat, breaking potatoes into chunks.

Instant Pot

VEGETABLES

ORANGE–SPICED GLAZED CARROTS

makes 6 servings

1 package (32 ounces) baby carrots

½ cup orange juice

⅓ cup packed brown sugar

3 tablespoons butter, cut into small pieces

¾ teaspoon ground cinnamon

½ teaspoon salt

¼ teaspoon ground nutmeg

¼ cup water

2 tablespoons cornstarch

Grated orange peel (optional)

Chopped fresh parsley (optional)

1. Combine carrots, orange juice, brown sugar, butter, cinnamon, salt and nutmeg in Instant Pot; mix well.

2. Secure lid and move pressure release valve to Sealing position. Press Pressure Cook or Manual; cook at high pressure 2 minutes.

3. When cooking is complete, use quick release.

4. Stir water into cornstarch in small bowl until smooth. Press Sauté; add cornstarch mixture to pot. Cook and stir 1 to 2 minutes or until sauce thickens. Garnish with orange peel and parsley.

QUICKER COLLARD GREENS

makes 4 to 6 servings

4 slices thick-cut bacon, cut into ½-inch pieces

1 pound collard greens, stems trimmed, roughly chopped

½ cup water or chicken broth

1 tablespoon cider vinegar

1 tablespoon packed brown sugar

¼ teaspoon salt

¼ teaspoon black pepper

¼ teaspoon red pepper flakes

1. Press Sauté; cook bacon in Instant Pot until crisp. Add half of greens; cook 1 minute or until greens begin to wilt, scraping up browned bits from bottom of pot. Add remaining greens; cook and stir 1 minute. Stir in water, vinegar, brown sugar, salt, black pepper and red pepper flakes; mix well.

2. Secure lid and move pressure release valve to Sealing position. Press Pressure Cook or Manual; cook at high pressure 20 minutes.

3. When cooking is complete, use quick release. Stir greens; serve warm.

CAULIFLOWER AND POTATO MASALA

makes 6 servings

1 tablespoon olive or vegetable oil

2 teaspoons minced garlic

1 teaspoon minced fresh ginger

1 teaspoon salt

1 teaspoon cumin seeds or ½ teaspoon ground cumin

1 teaspoon ground coriander

1 teaspoon garam masala

1 can (about 14 ounces) diced tomatoes

1 head cauliflower (about 1¼ pounds), broken into florets

1 pound red potatoes (2 large), peeled and cut into ½-inch wedges

2 tablespoons chopped fresh cilantro

1. Press Sauté; heat oil in Instant Pot. Add garlic, ginger, salt, cumin, coriander and garam masala; cook and stir about 30 seconds or until fragrant. Add tomatoes; cook and stir 1 minute. Add cauliflower and potatoes; mix well.

2. Secure lid and move pressure release valve to Sealing position. Press Pressure Cook or Manual; cook at high pressure 2 minutes.

3. When cooking is complete, use quick release. Sprinkle with cilantro.

BUTTERNUT SQUASH WITH APPLES, CRANBERRIES AND WALNUTS

makes 4 servings

1 tablespoon butter

1 medium Granny Smith apple, peeled and cut into ½-inch pieces

3 cups cubed peeled butternut squash (¾-inch pieces)

½ cup water

3 tablespoons dried cranberries

2 teaspoons packed brown sugar

½ teaspoon salt

¼ teaspoon ground cinnamon

⅛ teaspoon black pepper

2 tablespoons chopped walnuts

1. Press Sauté; melt butter in Instant Pot. Add apple; cook about 5 minutes or until tender, stirring occasionally. Remove to plate; set aside. Add squash, water, cranberries, brown sugar, salt, cinnamon and pepper to pot; stir until brown sugar is dissolved.

2. Secure lid and move pressure release valve to Sealing position. Press Pressure Cook or Manual; cook at high pressure 1 minute.

3. When cooking is complete, use quick release.

4. Press Sauté; add cooked apple to pot. Cook 2 minutes or until heated through, stirring occasionally. Gently stir in walnuts.

SPICED SWEET POTATOES

makes 4 to 6 servings

2½ pounds sweet potatoes, peeled and cut into ½-inch pieces

½ cup water

2 tablespoons dark brown sugar

1 teaspoon salt

1 teaspoon ground cinnamon

½ teaspoon ground nutmeg

2 tablespoons butter, cut into small pieces

½ teaspoon vanilla

1. Combine sweet potatoes, water, brown sugar, salt, cinnamon and nutmeg in Instant Pot; mix well.

2. Secure lid and move pressure release valve to Sealing position. Press Pressure Cook or Manual; cook at high pressure 3 minutes.

3. When cooking is complete, use quick release.

4. Press Sauté; add butter and vanilla to pot. Cook 1 to 2 minutes or until butter is melted, stirring gently to blend.

BEET AND ARUGULA SALAD

makes 6 servings

1 cup water

8 medium beets (5 to 6 ounces each)

⅓ cup red wine vinegar

¾ teaspoon salt

½ teaspoon black pepper

3 tablespoons extra virgin olive oil

1 package (5 ounces) baby arugula

1 package (4 ounces) goat cheese with garlic and herbs, crumbled

1. Pour water into Instant Pot; place rack in pot. Arrange beets on rack (or use steamer basket to hold beets). Secure lid and move pressure release valve to Sealing position. Press Pressure Cook or Manual; cook at high pressure 20 minutes.

2. When cooking is complete, use natural release for 10 minutes, then release remaining pressure. Set beets aside until cool enough to handle.

3. Meanwhile, whisk vinegar, salt and pepper in large bowl. Slowly add oil in thin, steady stream, whisking until well blended. Remove 3 tablespoons dressing to medium bowl.

4. Peel beets and cut into wedges. Add warm beets to large bowl; toss to coat with dressing. Add arugula to medium bowl; toss gently to coat with dressing. Place arugula on platter or plates, top with beets and cheese.

Instant Pot
VEGETABLES

PARMESAN POTATO WEDGES

makes 4 to 6 servings

- 2 pounds unpeeled red potatoes (about 6 medium), cut into ½-inch wedges
- ½ cup water
- ¼ cup finely chopped onion
- 2 tablespoons butter, cut into small pieces
- 1¼ teaspoons salt
- 1 teaspoon dried oregano
- ¼ teaspoon black pepper
- ¼ cup grated Parmesan cheese

1. Combine potatoes, water, onion, butter, salt, oregano and pepper in Instant Pot; mix well.

2. Secure lid and move pressure release valve to Sealing position. Press Pressure Cook or Manual; cook at high pressure 3 minutes.

3. When cooking is complete, use quick release. Transfer potatoes to serving platter; sprinkle with cheese.

Instant Pot

DESSERTS

BIG CHOCOLATE CHIP COOKIE

makes 6 to 8 servings

1 cup plus 2 tablespoons all-purpose flour

½ teaspoon baking soda

½ teaspoon salt

¼ cup (½ stick) butter, softened

½ cup packed brown sugar

2 tablespoons granulated sugar

1 egg

½ teaspoon vanilla

1 cup semisweet chocolate chunks or chips

1 cup water

1. Spray 7-inch metal cake pan with nonstick cooking spray. Combine flour, baking soda and salt in small bowl; mix well.

2. Beat butter, brown sugar and granulated sugar in medium bowl with electric mixer at medium speed until light and creamy. Add egg and vanilla; beat until well blended. Add flour mixture; beat just until blended. Stir in chocolate chunks. Spread batter in prepared pan. Cover pan with paper towel (to absorb moisture), making sure paper towel does not touch batter. Cover pan with foil over paper towel.

3. Pour water into Instant Pot; place rack in pot. Place pan on rack. Secure lid and move pressure release valve to Sealing position. Press Pressure Cook or Manual; cook at high pressure 35 minutes.

4. When cooking is complete, use natural release for 10 minutes, then release remaining pressure. Remove pan from pot. Uncover; cool on wire rack 15 minutes. Invert cookie onto plate; invert again onto serving plate. Serve warm or at room temperature.

PUMPKIN BREAD PUDDING

makes 4 servings

1 cup whole milk

2 eggs

½ cup canned pumpkin

⅓ cup packed brown sugar

1 tablespoon butter, melted

1½ teaspoons ground cinnamon

1 teaspoon vanilla

¼ teaspoon salt

¼ teaspoon ground nutmeg

8 slices cinnamon raisin bread, torn into small pieces (about 4 cups)

1¼ cups water

Bourbon Caramel Sauce (recipe follows, optional)

1. Spray 6- to 7-inch (1½-quart) soufflé dish or round baking dish with nonstick cooking spray. Whisk milk, eggs, pumpkin, brown sugar, butter, cinnamon, vanilla, salt and nutmeg in large bowl until well blended. Add bread cubes; stir gently to coat. Pour into prepared soufflé dish; cover with foil.

2. Pour water into Instant Pot; place rack in pot. Place soufflé dish on rack.

3. Secure lid and move pressure release valve to Sealing position. Press Pressure Cook or Manual; cook at high pressure 40 minutes.

4. When cooking is complete, use natural release for 10 minutes, then release remaining pressure.

5. Remove soufflé dish from pot. Uncover; cool 15 minutes. Meanwhile, prepare Bourbon Caramel Sauce, if desired. Serve bread pudding warm with sauce.

BOURBON CARAMEL SAUCE: Combine ¼ cup (½ stick) butter, ¼ cup packed brown sugar and ¼ cup whipping cream in small saucepan; bring to a boil over high heat, stirring frequently. Remove from heat; stir in 1 tablespoon bourbon.

CHOCOLATE TRUFFLE CAKE

makes 8 servings

Unsweetened cocoa
    powder

12 ounces bittersweet (60%)
    chocolate, chopped

½ cup (1 stick) butter, cut
    into small pieces

5 eggs, separated

1 teaspoon vanilla

¼ teaspoon salt

½ cup granulated sugar

1½ cups water

Powdered sugar and
    fresh raspberries
    (optional)

1. Spray 7-inch springform pan with nonstick cooking spray; dust with cocoa.

2. Combine chocolate and butter in large microwavable bowl; microwave on MEDIUM (50%) 2 minutes or until melted and smooth, stirring after each minute. Set aside to cool 5 minutes. Beat egg yolks and vanilla into chocolate mixture until well blended.

3. Beat egg whites and salt in medium bowl with electric mixer at medium speed until frothy. Slowly add granulated sugar, beating at medium-high speed until almost firm (but not stiff) peaks form. Fold one third of egg whites into chocolate mixture until blended. Gently fold in remaining egg whites just until blended. Spread batter in prepared pan; smooth top.

4. Pour water into Instant Pot; place rack in pot. Place pan on rack. Secure lid and move pressure release valve to Sealing position. Press Pressure Cook or Manual; cook at high pressure 15 minutes.

5. When cooking is complete, use natural release for 10 minutes, then release remaining pressure. Remove pan from pot. Cool in pan on wire rack 30 minutes; refrigerate at least 2 hours before serving. Remove side of pan; garnish with powdered sugar and raspberries.

QUICK AND EASY KHEER (INDIAN RICE PUDDING)

makes 6 to 8 servings

3 cups whole milk

²/₃ cup sugar

1 cup uncooked basmati rice, rinsed and drained

¹/₂ cup golden raisins

3 whole green cardamom pods or ¹/₄ teaspoon ground cardamon

¹/₄ teaspoon salt

Grated orange peel (optional)

Pistachio nuts (optional)

1. Combine milk and sugar in Instant Pot; stir until sugar is dissolved. Add rice, raisins, cardamom and salt; mix well.

2. Secure lid and move pressure release valve to Sealing position. Press Pressure Cook or Manual; cook at high pressure 5 minutes.

3. When cooking is complete, use natural release for 10 minutes, then release remaining pressure.

4. Stir rice pudding well before serving. (Pudding will thicken upon standing.) Garnish with orange peel and pistachios.

CLASSIC CHEESECAKE

makes 8 servings

½ cup graham cracker crumbs

½ cup plus 1 tablespoon sugar, divided

2 tablespoons butter, melted

2 packages (8 ounces each) cream cheese, softened

2 eggs, at room temperature

1 teaspoon vanilla

1½ cups water

1. Cut parchment paper to fit bottom of 7-inch springform pan. Lightly spray bottom and side of pan with nonstick cooking spray. Wrap outside of pan with foil.

2. Combine graham cracker crumbs, 1 tablespoon sugar and melted butter in small bowl; mix well. Pat mixture onto bottom of prepared pan. Freeze 10 minutes.

3. Beat cream cheese in large bowl with electric mixer at medium-high speed until smooth and creamy. Add remaining ½ cup sugar; beat about 3 minutes or until light and fluffy. Add eggs, one at a time, beating well after each addition. Stir in vanilla. Pour batter over prepared crust. Cover pan with foil.

4. Pour water into Instant Pot; place rack in pot. Place pan on rack. Secure lid and move pressure release valve to Sealing position. Press Pressure Cook or Manual; cook at high pressure 33 minutes.

5. When cooking is complete, use quick release. Remove pan from pot. Uncover; cool on wire rack 1 hour. Run thin knife around edge of cheesecake to loosen (do not remove side of pan). Refrigerate 2 to 3 hours or overnight.

RICH CHOCOLATE PUDDING

makes 6 servings

1½ **cups whipping cream**

4 **ounces bittersweet chocolate, chopped**

4 **egg yolks**

⅓ **cup packed brown sugar**

1 **tablespoon unsweetened cocoa powder**

1 **teaspoon vanilla**

¼ **teaspoon salt**

1¼ **cups water**

1. Heat cream to a simmer in medium saucepan over medium heat. Remove from heat. Add chocolate; stir until chocolate is melted and mixture is smooth.

2. Whisk egg yolks, brown sugar, cocoa, vanilla and salt in large bowl until well blended. Gradually add warm chocolate mixture, whisking constantly until blended. Strain mixture into 6- to 7-inch (1½-quart) soufflé dish or round baking dish; cover with foil.

3. Pour water into Instant Pot; place rack in pot. Place soufflé dish on rack.

4. Secure lid and move pressure release valve to Sealing position. Press Pressure Cook or Manual; cook at low pressure 22 minutes.

5. When cooking is complete, use natural release for 5 minutes, then release remaining pressure. Remove soufflé dish from pot. Uncover; cool to room temperature. Cover and refrigerate at least 3 hours or up to 2 days.

SUPERFAST APPLESAUCE

makes 4 cups

2 pounds (about 4 medium) sweet apples (such as Fuji, Gala or Honeycrisp), peeled and cut into 1-inch pieces

2 pounds (about 4 medium) Granny Smith apples, peeled and cut into 1-inch pieces

⅓ cup water

2 to 4 tablespoons packed brown sugar, divided

1 tablespoon lemon juice

1 teaspoon ground cinnamon

⅛ teaspoon salt

⅛ teaspoon ground nutmeg

⅛ teaspoon ground cloves

1. Combine apples, water, 2 tablespoons brown sugar, lemon juice, cinnamon, salt, nutmeg and cloves in Instant Pot; mix well.

2. Secure lid and move pressure release valve to Sealing position. Press Pressure Cook or Manual; cook at high pressure 4 minutes.

3. When cooking is complete, use quick release.

4. Stir applesauce; taste for seasoning and add remaining 2 tablespoons brown sugar, if desired. If there is excess liquid in pot, press Sauté and cook 2 to 3 minutes or until liquid evaporates. Cool completely before serving.

PLUM BREAD PUDDING

makes 6 servings

6 cups cubed brioche, egg bread or challah (1-inch cubes)

1½ tablespoons butter

2 large plums, pitted and cut into thin wedges

⅓ cup plus ½ tablespoon sugar, divided

3 eggs

¾ cup half-and-half

½ cup milk

½ teaspoon vanilla

¼ teaspoon salt

¼ teaspoon ground cinnamon

1¼ cups water

Whipping cream or vanilla ice cream (optional)

1. Preheat oven to 400°F. Spray 6- to 7-inch (1½-quart) soufflé dish or round baking dish with nonstick cooking spray.

2. Spread bread cubes in single layer on ungreased baking sheet. Bake 6 to 7 minutes or until lightly toasted, stirring halfway through baking time.

3. Meanwhile, melt butter in large skillet over medium-high heat. Add plums and ½ tablespoon sugar; cook 2 minutes or until plums are softened and release juices. Beat eggs in large bowl. Add half-and-half, milk, remaining ⅓ cup sugar, vanilla, salt and cinnamon; mix well. Add plums and toasted bread cubes; stir gently to coat. Pour into prepared soufflé dish; cover with foil.

4. Pour water into Instant Pot; place rack in pot. Place soufflé dish on rack. Secure lid and move pressure release valve to Sealing position. Press Pressure Cook or Manual; cook at high pressure 35 minutes.

5. When cooking is complete, use natural release for 10 minutes, then release remaining pressure. Remove soufflé dish from pot. Let stand, covered, 15 minutes. Uncover; serve warm with cream, if desired.

PUMPKIN CHOCOLATE CHIP CAKE

makes 8 servings

1½ cups all-purpose flour

1 teaspoon pumpkin pie spice

½ teaspoon baking powder

½ teaspoon baking soda

½ teaspoon salt

¼ teaspoon ground cinnamon

1 cup canned pumpkin

1 cup packed brown sugar

2 eggs

⅓ cup vegetable or canola oil

½ teaspoon vanilla

¾ cup mini semisweet chocolate chips

1½ cups water

Chocolate Glaze (recipe follows, optional)

1. Spray 6-cup bundt pan with nonstick cooking spray. Combine flour, pumpkin pie spice, baking powder, baking soda, salt and cinnamon in small bowl; mix well.

2. Whisk pumpkin, brown sugar, eggs, oil and vanilla in medium bowl until well blended. Add flour mixture; stir just until blended. Stir in chocolate chips. Pour batter into prepared pan; cover with foil.

3. Pour water into Instant Pot; place rack in pot. Place pan on rack. Secure lid and move pressure release valve to Sealing position. Press Pressure Cook or Manual; cook at high pressure 30 minutes.

4. When cooking is complete, use natural release for 10 minutes, then release remaining pressure. Remove pan from pot. Uncover; cool on wire rack 10 minutes. Invert cake onto serving plate; cool completely.

5. Prepare Chocolate Glaze, if desired; drizzle glaze over cake. Let stand until set.

CHOCOLATE GLAZE: Combine ¼ cup mini semisweet chocolate chips, 1 tablespoon butter and 2 teaspoons light corn syrup in small microwavable bowl or glass measuring cup. Microwave on MEDIUM (50% power) 1 minute; stir. Microwave 20 seconds; stir until mixture is melted and smooth.

SOUTHERN SWEET POTATO CUSTARD

makes 4 servings

1 can (16 ounces) cut sweet potatoes, drained

1 can (12 ounces) evaporated milk, divided

½ cup packed brown sugar

2 eggs

1 teaspoon ground cinnamon

½ teaspoon ground ginger

¼ teaspoon salt

1¼ cups water

Whipped cream (optional)

Ground nutmeg (optional)

1. Combine sweet potatoes and ¼ cup evaporated milk in food processor or blender; process until smooth. Add remaining evaporated milk, brown sugar, eggs, cinnamon, ginger and salt; process until well blended. Pour into 6- to 7-inch (1½-quart) soufflé dish or round baking dish; cover with foil.

2. Pour water into Instant Pot; place rack in pot. Place soufflé dish on rack.

3. Secure lid and move pressure release valve to Sealing position. Press Pressure Cook or Manual; cook at high pressure 40 minutes.

4. When cooking is complete, use natural release for 10 minutes, then release remaining pressure. Remove soufflé dish from pot. Uncover; cool 30 minutes. Garnish with whipped cream and nutmeg.

FUDGY DOUBLE CHOCOLATE BROWNIES

makes 8 servings

½ cup (1 stick) butter

¾ cup unsweetened cocoa powder

1 cup sugar

2 eggs

⅔ cup all-purpose flour

½ teaspoon salt

½ cup semisweet chocolate chunks or chips

1½ cups water

Vanilla ice cream (optional)

1. Spray 7-inch metal cake pan with nonstick cooking spray. Line bottom of pan with parchment paper; spray with cooking spray. Place butter in medium microwavable bowl; microwave until melted. Stir in cocoa until well blended.

2. Beat sugar and eggs in large bowl until well blended. Add cocoa mixture; stir until smooth. Add flour and salt; stir just until blended. Stir in chocolate chunks. Spread batter in prepared pan; smooth top. Cover pan with paper towel (to absorb moisture), making sure paper towel does not touch batter. Cover pan with foil over paper towel.

3. Pour water into Instant Pot; place rack in pot. Place pan on rack. Secure lid and move pressure release valve to Sealing position. Press Pressure Cook or Manual; cook at high pressure 24 minutes.

4. When cooking is complete, use natural release for 10 minutes, then release remaining pressure. Remove pan from pot. Uncover; cool on wire rack at least 10 minutes before serving. Invert brownie onto plate; remove parchment paper. Invert again onto serving plate. Serve warm or at room temperature with ice cream, if desired.

PEANUT BUTTER PUDDING

makes 6 servings

2 cups milk

2 eggs

⅓ cup creamy peanut butter

¼ cup packed brown sugar

¼ teaspoon vanilla

1 cup water

Shaved chocolate or shredded coconut (optional)

1. Spray six 3-ounce ramekins or custard cups with nonstick cooking spray. Combine milk, eggs, peanut butter, brown sugar and vanilla in blender; blend at high speed 1 minute. Pour into prepared ramekins. Cover each ramekin tightly with foil.

2. Pour water into Instant Pot; place rack in pot. Arrange ramekins on rack, stacking as necessary.

3. Secure lid and move pressure release valve to Sealing position. Press Pressure Cook or Manual; cook at high pressure 8 minutes.

4. When cooking is complete, use natural release for 10 minutes, then release remaining pressure.

5. Remove ramekins from pot. Uncover; cool to room temperature. Refrigerate until chilled. Garnish with shaved chocolate.

Instant Pot®

PRESSURE COOKING TIMES

MEAT	MINUTES UNDER PRESSURE	PRESSURE	RELEASE
Beef, Bone-in Short Ribs	35 to 45	High	Natural
Beef, Brisket	60 to 75	High	Natural
Beef, Ground	8	High	Natural
Beef, Roast (round, rump or shoulder)	60 to 70	High	Natural
Beef, Stew Meat	20 to 25	High	Natural or Quick
Lamb, Chops	5 to 10	High	Quick
Lamb, Leg or Shanks	35 to 40	High	Natural
Lamb, Stew Meat	12 to 15	High	Quick
Pork, Baby Back Ribs	25 to 30	High	Natural
Pork, Chops	7 to 10	High	Quick
Pork, Ground	5	High	Quick
Pork, Loin	15 to 25	High	Natural
Pork, Shoulder or Butt	45 to 60	High	Natural
Pork, Stew Meat	15 to 20	High	Quick

Instant Pot

POULTRY

	MINUTES UNDER PRESSURE	PRESSURE	RELEASE
Chicken Breasts, Bone-in	7 to 10	High	Quick
Chicken Breasts, Boneless	5 to 8	High	Quick
Chicken Thigh, Bone-in	10 to 14	High	Natural
Chicken Thigh, Boneless	8 to 10	High	Natural
Chicken Wings	10 to 12	High	Quick
Chicken, Whole	22 to 26	High	Natural
Eggs, Hard-Cooked (3 to 12)	9	Low	Quick
Turkey Breast, Bone-in	25 to 30	High	Natural
Turkey Breast, Boneless	15 to 20	High	Natural
Turkey Legs	35 to 40	High	Natural
Turkey, Ground	8 to 10	High	Quick

SEAFOOD

	MINUTES UNDER PRESSURE	PRESSURE	RELEASE
Cod	2 to 3	Low	Quick
Crab	2 to 3	Low	Quick
Halibut	6	Low	Quick
Mussels	1 to 2	Low	Quick
Salmon	4 to 5	Low	Quick
Scallops	1	Low	Quick
Shrimp	2 to 3	Low	Quick
Swordfish	4 to 5	Low	Quick
Tilapia	3	Low	Quick

Instant Pot
PRESSURE COOKING TIMES

DRIED BEANS AND LEGUMES

	UNSOAKED	SOAKED	PRESSURE	RELEASE
Black Beans	22 to 25	8 to 10	High	Natural
Black-Eyed Peas	9 to 11	3 to 5	High	Natural
Cannellini Beans	30 to 35	8 to 10	High	Natural
Chickpeas	35 to 40	18 to 22	High	Natural
Great Northern Beans	25 to 30	7 to 10	High	Natural
Kidney Beans	20 to 25	8 to 12	High	Natural
Lentils, Brown or Green	10 to 12	n/a	High	Natural
Lentils, Red or Yellow Split	1	n/a	High	Natural
Navy Beans	20 to 25	7 to 8	High	Natural
Pinto Beans	22 to 25	8 to 10	High	Natural
Split Peas	8 to 10	n/a	High	Natural

GRAINS

	LIQUID PER CUP	MINUTES UNDER PRESSURE	PRESSURE	RELEASE
Barley, Pearl	2	18 to 22	High	Natural
Barley, Whole	2½	30 to 35	High	Natural
Bulgur	3	8	High	Natural
Farro	2	10 to 12	High	Natural
Grits, Medium	4	12 to 15	High	10 minute natural
Millet	1½	1	High	Natural
Oats, Rolled	2	4 to 5	High	10 minute natural
Oats, Steel-Cut	3	10 to 13	High	10 minute natural
Quinoa	1½	1	High	10 minute natural
Polenta, Instant	3	5	High	5 minute natural
Rice, Arborio	2	6 to 7	High	Quick
Rice, Brown	1	22	High	10 minute natural
Rice, White Long Grain	1	4	High	10 minute natural

Instant Pot
PRESSURE COOKING TIMES

VEGETABLES	MINUTES UNDER PRESSURE	PRESSURE	RELEASE
Artichokes, Whole	9 to 12	High	Natural
Beets, Medium Whole	18 to 24	High	Quick
Brussels Sprouts, Whole	2 to 3	High	Quick
Cabbage, Sliced	3 to 5	High	Quick
Carrots, Sliced	2 to 4	High	Quick
Cauliflower, Florets	2 to 3	High	Quick
Cauliflower, Whole	3 to 5	High	Quick
Corn on the Cob	2 to 4	High	Quick
Eggplant	3 to 4	High	Quick
Fennel, Sliced	3 to 4	High	Quick
Green Beans	2 to 4	High	Quick
Kale	3	High	Quick
Leeks	3	High	Quick
Okra	3	High	Quick
Potatoes, Baby or Fingerling	6 to 10	High	Natural
Potatoes, New	7 to 9	High	Natural
Potatoes, 1-inch pieces	4 to 6	High	Quick
Potatoes, Sweet, 1-inch pieces	3	High	Quick
Potatoes, Sweet, Whole	8 to 12	High	Natural
Spinach	1	High	Quick
Squash, Acorn, Halved	7	High	Natural
Squash, Butternut, 1-inch pieces	4 to 6	High	Quick
Squash, Spaghetti, Halved	6 to 10	High	Natural
Tomatoes, cut into pieces for sauce	5	High	Natural

Instant Pot
INDEX

A

Apple-Cinnamon Breakfast Risotto, 22
Artichoke Dijon Chicken Thighs, 84
Asian Chicken and Noodles, 175
Asparagus Risotto, 160
Asparagus-Spinach Risotto, 160

B

Bacon
Bacon and Stout Short Ribs, 102
Frijoles Borrachos (Drunken Beans), 172
Pork and Cabbage Soup, 44
Quicker Collard Greens, 212
Savory Cod Stew, 34
Shortcut Baked Beans, 158
Split Pea Soup, 58
Sweet and Sour Red Cabbage, 202
Tex-Mex Chili, 112
Warm Potato Salad, 197
Bacon and Stout Short Ribs, 102
Barbecue Beef Sandwiches, 93
Barley
Barley with Currants and Pine Nuts, 152
Fruity Whole Grain Cereal, 18
Mushroom Barley Soup, 48
Barley with Currants and Pine Nuts, 152
Beans *(see also individual listings)*
Quick Spaghetti Supper, 186
Simple Sloppy Joes, 106
White Beans and Tomatoes, 145

Beans, Black
Beef Fajita Soup, 120
Quick Chicken and Bean Stew, 46
Salsa Verde Chicken Stew, 42
Sweet Potato and Black Bean Chili, 150
Beans, Great Northern
Chili Verde, 130
Quick Chicken and Bean Stew, 46
Vegetable Bean Soup, 52
Beans, Green
Creole-Spiced Pot Roast, 98
Spicy Asian Green Beans, 206
Beans, Kidney
Campfire Sausage and Potato Soup, 40
Chorizo Burritos, 128
Southwestern Corn and Beans, 164
Taco Salad, 94
Beans, Pinto
Beef Fajita Soup, 120
Frijoles Borrachos (Drunken Beans), 172
Hearty Chicken Chili, 72
Shortcut Baked Beans, 158
Taco Salad, 94
Beef
Bacon and Stout Short Ribs, 102
Barbecue Beef Sandwiches, 93
Beef Fajita Soup, 120
Beef Stew with a Coffee Kick, 104
Corned Beef and Cabbage, 116
Creole-Spiced Pot Roast, 98
Greek Beef Stew, 38
Italian Beef Ragu, 96
Italian Beef Sandwiches, 114

Beef *(continued)*
Southwestern Chile Beef, 118
Sweet and Savory Brisket, 108
Tex-Mex Chili, 112
Beef Fajita Soup, 120
Beef, Ground
Easy Meatballs, 100
Instant Chili Mac, 194
Meat Loaf, 110
Quick Spaghetti Supper, 186
Simple Sloppy Joes, 106
Taco Salad, 94
Beef Stew with a Coffee Kick, 104
Beet and Arugula Salad, 220
Berry Compote, 30
Big Chocolate Chip Cookie, 225
Bourbon Caramel Sauce, 226
Bulgur Pilaf with Caramelized Onions and Kale, 156
Butter Chicken, 70
Butternut Squash with Apples, Cranberries and Walnuts, 216

C

Campfire Sausage and Potato Soup, 40
Cauliflower and Potato Masala, 214
Cheesy Polenta, 146
Chicken
Artichoke Dijon Chicken Thighs, 84
Asian Chicken and Noodles, 175
Butter Chicken, 70
Chicken Adobo, 74
Chicken Enchilada Chili, 90
Coconut Curry Chicken Soup, 36

Instant Pot
INDEX

Chicken *(continued)*
Curried Chicken and Winter Vegetable Stew, 54
Hearty Chicken Chili, 72
Hoisin Barbecue Chicken Sliders, 76
Indian-Style Apricot Chicken, 80
One-Pot Chinese Chicken Soup, 62
Provençal Lemon and Olive Chicken, 88
Quick Chicken and Bean Stew, 46
Rotisserie-Style Chicken, 66
Salsa Verde Chicken Stew, 42
Spanish Chicken and Rice, 78
Tuesday Night Tacos, 65
Chicken Adobo, 74
Chicken Enchilada Chili, 90

Chickpeas
Chickpea Tikka Masala, 168
Pasta e Ceci, 184
Spicy African Chickpea and Sweet Potato Stew, 60
Chickpea Tikka Masala, 168

Chilies
Chicken Enchilada Chili, 90
Chili Verde, 130
Hearty Chicken Chili, 72
Instant Chili Mac, 194
Sweet Potato and Black Bean Chili, 150
Taco Salad, 94
Tex-Mex Chili, 112
Chili-Spiced Pork Loin, 124
Chili Verde, 130
Chili Wagon Wheel Pasta, 178
Chipotle BBQ Turkey Sandwiches, 86

Chocolate
Big Chocolate Chip Cookie, 225
Chocolate Glaze, 240
Chocolate Truffle Cake, 228
Fudgy Double Chocolate Brownies, 244
Pumpkin Chocolate Chip Cake, 240
Rich Chocolate Pudding, 234
Chocolate Glaze, 240
Chocolate Truffle Cake, 228
Chorizo Burritos, 128
Chunky Ranch Potatoes, 208
Cider Pork and Onions, 136
Classic Cheesecake, 232
Classic Irish Oatmeal, 30
Classic Macaroni and Cheese, 180
Coconut Curry Chicken Soup, 36

Corn
Chicken Enchilada Chili, 90
Chorizo Burritos, 128
Creole-Spiced Pot Roast, 98
Jerk Pork and Sweet Potato Stew, 142
Quick Shrimp and Okra Stew, 50
Salsa Verde Chicken Stew, 42
Southwestern Corn and Beans, 164
Corned Beef and Cabbage, 116
Creamy Tomato Soup, 33
Creole-Spiced Pot Roast, 98
Crustless Spinach Quiche, 24
Curried Chicken and Winter Vegetable Stew, 54

E
Easy Cheesy Lasagna, 176
Easy Meatballs, 100

Eggs
Crustless Spinach Quiche, 24
Kale and Roasted Pepper Frittata, 14
Shakshuka, 198

F
Farro Risotto with Mushrooms and Spinach, 148
Focaccia Croutons, 33
French Toast Casserole, 16
Frijoles Borrachos (Drunken Beans), 172
Fruit Chutney, 124
Fruity Whole Grain Cereal, 18
Fudgy Double Chocolate Brownies, 244

G
Garlic Parmesan Spaghetti Squash, 204
Greek Beef Stew, 38
Greek Rice, 154

H
Hearty Chicken Chili, 72
Herb Lemon Turkey Breast, 82
Hoisin Barbecue Chicken Sliders, 76
Honey Ginger Ribs, 134
Hot and Sweet Sausage Sandwiches, 138

I
Indian-Style Apricot Chicken, 80
Instant Chili Mac, 194
Italian Beef Ragu, 96
Italian Beef Sandwiches, 114

J
Jalapeño-Cheddar Corn Bread, 162
Jerk Pork and Sweet Potato Stew, 142

Instant Pot

INDEX

K

Kale

Bulgur Pilaf with Caramelized Onions and Kale, 156

Kale and Roasted Pepper Frittata, 14

Kale and Roasted Pepper Frittata, 14

L

Lemon Blueberry Oatmeal, 12

Lentil Bolognese, 192

M

Mashed Sweet Potatoes and Parsnips, 200

Meat Loaf, 110

Mushroom Barley Soup, 48

Mushrooms

Artichoke Dijon Chicken Thighs, 84

Creole-Spiced Pot Roast, 98

Farro Risotto with Mushrooms and Spinach, 148

Lentil Bolognese, 192

Mushroom Barley Soup, 48

Turkey Vegetable Rice Soup, 56

O

One-Pot Chinese Chicken Soup, 62

One-Pot Pasta with Sausage, 190

Orange-Spiced Glazed Carrots, 210

P

Pancake Breakfast Casserole, 28

Parmesan Garlic Monkey Bread, 11

Parmesan Potato Wedges, 222

Pasta

Asian Chicken and Noodles, 175

Chili Wagon Wheel Pasta, 178

Classic Macaroni and Cheese, 180

Easy Cheesy Lasagna, 176

Instant Chili Mac, 194

Lentil Bolognese, 192

One-Pot Chinese Chicken Soup, 62

One-Pot Pasta with Sausage, 190

Pasta e Ceci, 184

Penne with Ricotta, Tomatoes and Basil, 188

Quick Spaghetti Supper, 186

Spicy Sausage and Penne Pasta, 182

Pasta e Ceci, 184

Peanut Butter Pudding, 246

Penne with Ricotta, Tomatoes and Basil, 188

Perfect BBQ Ribs, 123

Pesto Turkey Meatballs, 68

Plum Bread Pudding, 238

Pork

Chili-Spiced Pork Loin, 124

Chili Verde, 130

Cider Pork and Onions, 136

Honey Ginger Ribs, 134

Jerk Pork and Sweet Potato Stew, 142

Perfect BBQ Ribs, 123

Pork and Cabbage Soup, 44

Pork Picadillo, 126

Pork Roast with Fruit, 140

Pulled Pork Sandwiches, 132

Pork and Cabbage Soup, 44

Pork Picadillo, 126

Pork Roast with Fruit, 140

Potatoes

Beef Stew with a Coffee Kick, 104

Campfire Sausage and Potato Soup, 40

Cauliflower and Potato Masala, 214

Chunky Ranch Potatoes, 208

Parmesan Potato Wedges, 222

Savory Cod Stew, 34

Vegetable Bean Soup, 52

Warm Potato Salad, 197

Provençal Lemon and Olive Chicken, 88

Pulled Pork Sandwiches, 132

Pumpkin Bread Pudding, 226

Pumpkin Chocolate Chip Cake, 240

Pumpkin Risotto, 170

Q

Quick and Easy Kheer (Indian Rice Pudding), 230

Quick Chicken and Bean Stew, 46

Quicker Collard Greens, 212

Quick Shrimp and Okra Stew, 50

Quick Spaghetti Supper, 186

R

Rice

Apple-Cinnamon Breakfast Risotto, 22

Asparagus Risotto, 160

Asparagus-Spinach Risotto, 160

Chorizo Burritos, 128

Fruity Whole Grain Cereal, 18

Greek Rice, 154

Pumpkin Risotto, 170

Quick and Easy Kheer (Indian Rice Pudding), 230

Instant Pot
INDEX

Rice (continued)
Spanish Chicken and Rice, 78
Spanish Rice, 166
Turkey Vegetable Rice Soup, 56
Rich Chocolate Pudding, 234
Rotisserie-Style Chicken, 66

S
Salsa Verde Chicken Stew, 42
Sausage
Campfire Sausage and Potato Soup, 40
Chorizo Burritos, 128
Hot and Sweet Sausage Sandwiches, 138
One-Pot Pasta with Sausage, 190
Spanish Chicken and Rice, 78
Spicy Sausage and Penne Pasta, 182
Savory Cod Stew, 34
Seafood
Quick Shrimp and Okra Stew, 50
Savory Cod Stew, 34
Shakshuka, 198
Shortcut Baked Beans, 158
Simple Sloppy Joes, 106
Soups
Beef Fajita Soup, 120
Campfire Sausage and Potato Soup, 40
Coconut Curry Chicken Soup, 36
Creamy Tomato Soup, 33
Mushroom Barley Soup, 48
One-Pot Chinese Chicken Soup, 62
Pork and Cabbage Soup, 44
Split Pea Soup, 58
Turkey Vegetable Rice Soup, 56
Vegetable Bean Soup, 52

Southern Sweet Potato Custard, 242
Southwestern Chile Beef, 118
Southwestern Corn and Beans, 164
Spanish Chicken and Rice, 78
Spanish Rice, 166
Spiced Sweet Potatoes, 218
Spice Paste, 60
Spicy African Chickpea and Sweet Potato Stew, 60
Spicy Asian Green Beans, 206
Spicy Sausage and Penne Pasta, 182
Spinach
Asparagus-Spinach Risotto, 160
Crustless Spinach Quiche, 24
Farro Risotto with Mushrooms and Spinach, 148
Split Pea Soup, 58
Stews
Beef Stew with a Coffee Kick, 104
Curried Chicken and Winter Vegetable Stew, 54
Greek Beef Stew, 38
Quick Chicken and Bean Stew, 46
Quick Shrimp and Okra Stew, 50
Salsa Verde Chicken Stew, 42
Savory Cod Stew, 34
Spicy African Chickpea and Sweet Potato Stew, 60
Sticky Cinnamon Monkey Bread, 20
Superfast Applesauce, 236
Superfood Breakfast Porridge, 26

Sweet and Savory Brisket, 108
Sweet and Sour Red Cabbage, 202
Sweet Potato and Black Bean Chili, 150
Sweet Potatoes
Jerk Pork and Sweet Potato Stew, 142
Mashed Sweet Potatoes and Parsnips, 200
Southern Sweet Potato Custard, 242
Spiced Sweet Potatoes, 218
Spicy African Chickpea and Sweet Potato Stew, 60
Sweet and Savory Brisket, 108
Sweet Potato and Black Bean Chili, 150

T
Taco Salad, 94
Tex-Mex Chili, 112
Turkey Vegetable Rice Soup, 56
Tuesday Night Tacos, 65
Turkey
Chili Wagon Wheel Pasta, 178
Chipotle BBQ Turkey Sandwiches, 86
Herb Lemon Turkey Breast, 82
Pesto Turkey Meatballs, 68
Turkey Vegetable Rice Soup, 56

V
Vegetable Bean Soup, 52

W
Warm Potato Salad, 197
White Beans and Tomatoes, 145

Instant Pot

VOLUME MEASUREMENTS (dry)

1/8 teaspoon = 0.5 mL
1/4 teaspoon = 1 mL
1/2 teaspoon = 2 mL
3/4 teaspoon = 4 mL
1 teaspoon = 5 mL
1 tablespoon = 15 mL
2 tablespoons = 30 mL
1/4 cup = 60 mL
1/3 cup = 75 mL
1/2 cup = 125 mL
2/3 cup = 150 mL
3/4 cup = 175 mL
1 cup = 250 mL
2 cups = 1 pint = 500 mL
3 cups = 750 mL
4 cups = 1 quart = 1 L

VOLUME MEASUREMENTS (fluid)

1 fluid ounce (2 tablespoons) = 30 mL
4 fluid ounces (1/2 cup) = 125 mL
8 fluid ounces (1 cup) = 250 mL
12 fluid ounces (1 1/2 cups) = 375 mL
16 fluid ounces (2 cups) = 500 mL

WEIGHTS (mass)

1/2 ounce = 15 g
1 ounce = 30 g
3 ounces = 90 g
4 ounces = 120 g
8 ounces = 225 g
10 ounces = 285 g
12 ounces = 360 g
16 ounces = 1 pound = 450 g

DIMENSIONS

1/16 inch = 2 mm
1/8 inch = 3 mm
1/4 inch = 6 mm
1/2 inch = 1.5 cm
3/4 inch = 2 cm
1 inch = 2.5 cm

OVEN TEMPERATURES

250°F = 120°C
275°F = 140°C
300°F = 150°C
325°F = 160°C
350°F = 180°C
375°F = 190°C
400°F = 200°C
425°F = 220°C
450°F = 230°C

BAKING PAN SIZES

Utensil	Size in Inches/Quarts	Metric Volume	Size in Centimeters
Baking or Cake Pan (square or rectangular)	8×8×2	2 L	20×20×5
	9×9×2	2.5 L	23×23×5
	12×8×2	3 L	30×20×5
	13×9×2	3.5 L	33×23×5
Loaf Pan	8×4×3	1.5 L	20×10×7
	9×5×3	2 L	23×13×7
Round Layer Cake Pan	8×1½	1.2 L	20×4
	9×1½	1.5 L	23×4
Pie Plate	8×1¼	750 mL	20×3
	9×1¼	1 L	23×3
Baking Dish or Casserole	1 quart	1 L	—
	1½ quart	1.5 L	—
	2 quart	2 L	—